Self-talk, Imagery, and Prayer in Counseling

RESOURCES FOR
CHRISTIAN COUNSELING

RESOURCES FOR CHRISTIAN COUNSELING

(Other volumes forthcoming.)

Self-talk, Imagery, and Prayer in Counseling

H. NORMAN WRIGHT

RESOURCES FOR CHRISTIAN COUNSELING

General Editor

Gary R. Collins, Ph.D.

WORD BOOKS
PUBLISHER
WACO, TEXAS

A DIVISION OF
WORD, INCORPORATED

Library of Congress Cataloging-in-Publication Data

Wright, H. Norman.
  Self-talk, imagery, and prayer in counseling.

  (Resources for Christian counseling; v. 3)
  Bibliography: p.
  Includes index.
  1. Pastoral counseling. 2. Counseling. 3. Imaginary conversations. 4. Imagery (Psychology) I. Title.
II. Series.
BV4012.2.W754   1986   253.5   86–19034
ISBN 0–8499–0585–0

6 7 8 9 8 FG 9 8 7 6 5 4 3 2 1
Printed in the United States of America

CONTENTS

EDITOR'S PREFACE

Do you talk to yourself? If you answer honestly, you would probably say yes. We all talk to ourselves silently (and sometimes out loud), especially when we are alone. We carry on mental self-talk conversations about our plans, our hopes, our activities, and our conclusions. And often we say things about ourselves that may be neither wise nor accurate.

I'm ugly, thinks the insecure teenager.

I'll never succeed in life, thinks another.

I'm too stupid to understand algebra, the student tells himself.

God will never forgive me, concludes another.

This is the kind of self-talk that creates problems, undercuts

7

self-esteem, builds prejudice, and sometimes leads to theological error.

But self-talk can also be beneficial. We can learn to tell ourselves things that build confidence, improve our skills, keep us from sin, give a more accurate picture of God, and build better interpersonal relationships.

Within recent years a number of books, both secular and Christian, have discussed the importance of self-talk in our daily living. Few have looked at the issue from a counseling perspective and even fewer have considered how self-talk can be used by Christian counselors. This is one of the goals of this book.

Nobody is better qualified than H. Norman Wright to discuss self-talk, and the related issues of imagery and prayer in counseling. Seminary professor, counselor, teacher, prolific writer, conference speaker, committed Christian—Norm Wright is all of these, and a family man in addition. He is widely known for his work in marital and premarital counseling, and has been on the forefront of creative approaches to Christian counseling.

As every counselor is well aware, we currently are living in the midst of a "counseling boom." Surely there has never been a time in history when so many people are aware of psychological issues, concerned about personal problems, interested in psychological writings, and willing to talk about their insecurities, inadequacies, and intimate concerns. Within only a few decades we have seen the birth of a great host of theories, degree programs, books, seminars, articles, new journals, radio programs, films, and tape presentations that deal with counseling-related issues. Numerous counselors have appeared, some with good training and great competence, but others with little sensitivity and not much awareness of what they are trying to accomplish.

Perhaps it is not surprising that the counseling field is confusing to many people, threatening to some, and often criticized both within the church and without. Nevertheless, people still struggle with psychological and spiritual problems, stress is both a personal and social issue, and many seek help from counselors.

And how does the counselor keep abreast of the latest developments? Many turn to books, but it is difficult to know which of the many volumes on the market are of good quality and which are not. The Resources for Christian Counseling Series is an attempt to provide books that give clearly written, practical, up-to-date overviews of the issues faced by contemporary Christian counselors. Written by counseling experts, each of whom has a strong Christian commitment, the books are intended to be examples of accurate psychology and careful use of Scripture. Each will have a clear evangelical perspective, careful documentation, a strong practical orientation, and freedom from the sweeping statements and undocumented rhetoric that sometimes characterize books in the counseling field. All of the Resources for Christian Counseling books will have similar bindings and together they will comprise a complete encyclopedia of Christian counseling.

Norman Wright's volume in this series tackles three significant but often ignored issues in Christian counseling. Helping people with their *self-talk*, as we have seen, has become an important topic within recent counseling literature. The use of *imagery* is controversial, especially in some Christian circles where a few critics have branded it as a solely secular technique. *Prayer*, in contrast, is widely recommended as a part of counseling, but almost nobody has discussed how this can be used most effectively in the helping process.

It takes a knowledgeable and experienced counselor to write about topics such as these. Norman Wright is that kind of counselor. His book is relevant, up-to-date, helpful, and biblical.

And the book is intensely practical. Not only does it discuss self-talk, imagery, and prayer, but it tells how each of these can be applied to a variety of counseling problems. In addition to the discussion of these issues, the following pages include a number of practical techniques and exercises that can be used, even before you finish reading the book.

If you read carefully you might also discover, as I did, that the conclusions about self-talk, imagery, and prayer can be applied not only to your counselees. You can apply them, with benefit, to yourself.

Gary R. Collins, Ph.D.
Kildeer, Illinois

INTRODUCTION

FOR THE PAST QUARTER OF A CENTURY, counseling has been a major part of my life. It has been an odyssey that has evolved through various stages. Initially, my counseling ministry began when I served among parents and adolescents as a minister of education and youth. The second stage of expression and development came while teaching and counseling prospective ministers enrolled in classes at Talbot Theological Seminary. The current phase, private practice, involves a clientele of both Christian laypeople and ministers.

The difficulties that are brought to my attention now as compared to that first decade of my experience have not changed all that much: they have just intensified and there are more of them. Every now and then some new aberration occurs, or a difficulty never before encountered plunges me into research and sends me seeking advice. But the ills, struggles, and needs of men and women that have been with us for centuries are still apparent, and will continue.

Perhaps you are where I was years ago, just starting out. Or you could be completing three decades of counseling others. Wherever you are in your journey of helping people unravel their problems and rebuild their lives, I trust that you are continually seeking to grow and develop your skills and proficiencies. No matter how long we have counseled, there is always more to learn.

What happens when individuals or couples come to see you for counseling? What happens when they leave your office? Is there hope and do they experience change, or are both they and you frustrated? Do you ever say, "How I wish I knew what to say and do?"

I wish I had known twenty-five years ago what I know now, but that is a wistful fantasy. For most of us, our schooling was not sufficient. Those going into the ministry take few courses in counseling in college, Bible school, or seminary. And because of the lack of time, most of these courses do not give students the specifics, the skill training, the practice, or the supervision needed. Professional counselors also recognize deficiencies in their schooling. But we can continue to grow and develop our abilities.

I have learned more about counseling after five years of graduate school than during that time, and you can too, through reading, practicing, seminars, discussion, specialized courses, observation, and by counseling others.

When I began, few books were available in this subject area and most held a liberal bent. Audio- and video-training tapes were lacking, as well as the now popular one- or two-day training seminars. But that has all changed. This may be a bold statement, but today there is little reason *not* to be equipped, given the wealth of resources available.

This book, Self-talk, Imagery, and Prayer in Counseling, is an expression of my current development in counseling. It is not the result of a few weeks of theoretical research, but several years of practice. I'm sure that the approach suggested here can be improved upon and I trust and pray that you, the reader, will be able to accomplish this improvement. Please be open in your thinking and flexible in your application of these approaches.

In this book, illustrations of counseling situations have been used with client permission, or the cases have been sufficiently altered to protect persons' identity.

I appreciate the assistance of my personal editorial consultant Marilyn McGinnis, my typist Jan Blakeslee, and the expressive and fun-loving editor of this series, Gary Collins. I am indebted to the many pioneers in the various approaches suggested in this book. Their written contributions are listed in the bibliography.

Because of this book and the others in this series and due to training opportunities and other resources available today, I pray that you will grow and develop into a skilled counselor in far less time than it has taken those of us who started out in the fifties and sixties.

Self-talk, Imagery,
and Prayer
in Counseling

RESOURCES FOR
CHRISTIAN COUNSELING

CHAPTER ONE

THE MOST IMPORTANT ELEMENT IN COUNSELING

THIRTY-FIVE OF THEM sat there in their chairs waiting for the class to begin. Most of them were young; a few were in their thirties and forties. Men and women, waiting for the instruction and the learning experience that was supposed to equip them to minister to the needs of hurting individuals and families.

There was some restless activity and some hushed talking. They were not sure what to expect, what the next few months would hold for them. This class was different from Hermeneutics, Greek, Biblical Theology, or New Testament Introduction. This was their one and only seminary course in counseling techniques—a course that was supposed to prepare them to listen, diagnose, discern, develop the proper response, and enable hurting people to change their lives and handle the upsets that come their way.

The students looked eager. In fact, some of them just couldn't wait to get out there and counsel people. A few had already made up their minds concerning the best way to counsel: Give advice, point out Scriptures from the Word of God, pray with the person, and see the counselee no more than once or twice! I hoped to change this perspective and suggest a more balanced approach. Other students were apprehensive, not knowing whether they really wanted to become involved in counseling at all.

A number of questions went through my mind: *I wonder what they will be thinking and feeling about counseling ten years from now. Will they still see it as a life-changing ministry, or will they be locked in the grip of discouragement? Are they ready to confront the misery of life's mysteries? I wonder how many of them will be shocked when they hear the problems of doubt, infidelity, abuse, incest, severe depression, betrayal, the agonizing cries of parents, and the never-ending difficulties which will be confided to them by members of their congregation.*

It was 10:30 A.M.—time to begin class. I stepped to the podium and looked out at this mixture of first-year seminary students, but before I could begin speaking, a student raised his hand and said,

Dr. Wright, there are two important questions I would like to have answered during this semester and I wanted to let you know about them right away. First of all, what is the most important element in counseling that will help me be effective? Second, what style of counseling is best to use in order to help bring about a significant and lasting change in a person's life? I don't want to waste either the counselee's time or mine. I hope my teaching and preaching will be somewhat effective and have an impact. But I would also like to see my counseling ministry have an impact as well. Could you work toward answering these questions for me and the others during this semester?

In a nutshell, that student summed up the purpose of this book: to provide you, the reader, with guidelines, structure, and helps so that your counseling ministry can be effective. Even though the main approach of this book is the use of self-talk, imagery, and prayer in counseling, the vital questions of this seminary student and the topic of chapter 2 must be considered first. Let us begin then with the first question—the most important element of counseling.

THE COUNSELOR IS KEY

The most important element in the counseling process is you! Yes, *you*, the person doing the counseling. That is not to negate the importance of the ministry of the Holy Spirit, or prayer, or the Word of God. What it does mean is that you, the counselor, either block the effectiveness of these other elements, or you are the vehicle that helps a person appropriate them for his or her life. The personal characteristics, beliefs, and behavior of the counseling minister are the most important determinants of the success of counseling. This does not mean that the minister is a model of perfection. Rather, it means that he or she is in the process of growing and changing and incorporating with the Holy Spirit's assistance those characteristics that produce maturity. Let's look at some of these important characteristics.

1. *A sincere interest in others.* You can't fake this one. There are some people who should not be involved in ministry or counseling since they lack this genuine interest. It is possible to have it at one time and see it diminish through the process of burnout.

In general, the way we relate to others will indicate if we respect, trust and value them. Our calling is to see in them the potential and value that God has for them. In counseling, such caring can be shown by giving support, exhibiting warmth and challenging them to look at ignored areas of their lives. We care for the counselee when our time is devoted to meeting their needs and concerns and not our own.

2. *The ability to be empathic.* This is the ability and willingness to be with the person emotionally and intellectually in his experience of joy or pain. The Scriptures tell us to weep with those who weep and rejoice with those who rejoice. In

order for this to happen, you must be an open person emotionally yourself. Unfortunately, many people (men, in particular) are emotionally handicapped because they have not developed the emotional side of their lives. They fear their emotions and are actually out of touch with them. This is the number one complaint I have heard over the past decade from wives as they have talked about marital concerns. (For additional information on this subject see the suggested reading list at the end of Appendix 2, p. 196.)

Empathy is a quality which we are called to have as believers. One of the purposes of empathy is the greater depth and enjoyment of life it opens up to us. Empathy means "to feel unto," or "to feel with." It is as though we are in the driver's seat with the other person, and feeling and sensing with him or her. It is viewing the situation through their eyes, and feeling as they feel at that moment. It involves being able to get inside the other person—looking at and getting a feel for what the world is like through his perspective. This means we need the ability to discriminate and to communicate our understanding to the other person in such a manner that he realizes we really do understand how he feels. It is being able to sense another person's joy, to understand what underlies that joy, and to let the person know that we are capturing that moment with him. In empathy we are not giving a diagnostic evaluation of the counselee but are simply understanding with him.

Empathy means developing the ability to go beyond factual knowledge and become involved in the person's world of feelings. But it also involves doing so without personally going through the full extent of what the other person is experiencing. If you try to do that you lose your objectivity and become overwhelmed. You cannot experience the identical emotions of a person; that would be overinvolvement. But it does mean focusing on the counselees' feelings and being with them at that time. How do you do this? By saying, "Oh, yeah. I know what you're feeling. Sure, everyone feels that way at one time or another"? No, it takes much more time than that.

For you to be seen as a person who cares and is sensitive and empathic, you need to use language that conveys that feeling. Repeating the same phrases over and over borders on redundancy. What you need is a repertoire of appropriate introductory phrases such as the following list of possible empathic response leads. Rehearse them again and again until you are comfortable with them and they are fixed in your own mind for later use.

Empathic Response Leads

"Kind of feeling . . ."
"Sort of feeling . . ."
"As I get it, you felt that . . ."
"I'm picking up that you . . ."
"Sort of a feeling that . . ."
"If I'm hearing you correctly . . ."
"To me it's almost like you are saying, I . . ."
"Sort of hear you saying that maybe you . . ."
"Kind of made (makes) you feel . . ."
"The thing you feel most right now is sort of like . . ."
"So, you feel . . ."
"What I hear you saying is . . ."
"So, as you see it . . ."
"As I get it, you're saying . . ."
"What I guess I'm hearing is . . ."
"I somehow sense that maybe you feel . . ."
"You feel . . ."
"I really hear you saying that . . ."
"I wonder if you're expressing concern that . . ."
"It sounds as if you're indicating you . . ."
"I wonder if you're saying . . ."
"You place a high value on . . ."
"It seems to you . . ."
"Like right now . . ."
"You often feel . . ."
"You feel, perhaps . . ."
"You appear to be feeling . . ."
"It appears you . . ."
"As I hear it, you . . ."
"So, from where you sit . . ."

"Your feeling now is that . . ."
"I read you as . . ."
"Sometimes you . . ."
"You must have felt . . ."
"I sense that you're feeling . . ."
"Very much feeling . . ."
"Your message seems to be, I . . ."
"You appear . . ."
"Listening to you, it seems as if . . ."
"I gather . . ."
"So your world is a place where you . . ."
"You communicate (convey) a sense of . . ."

Empathic statements not only respond to the counselee's surface feelings, but also focus on those deeper feelings that the person may not be expressing or may not be fully aware of at the time. Often, when a person is expressing anger, he or she is also feeling hurt. You can respond to both those feelings. These phrases are sometimes called *additive empathic* responses because they attempt to help the counselee put deeper feelings into words. They do require the counselor to make an inference. Statements like these are not stated as definite fact, but in a very *tentative* manner. This allows the counselee to accept or reject the possibility of the statement. It allows him or her to say that part of your response was accurate and part inaccurate. Some phrases might be:

"It sounds as if . . ."
"I'm wondering if you're saying . . ."
"Perhaps . . ."
"Maybe . . ."
"Is it possible that . . ."
"Would this fit . . ."
"Do you suppose . . ." [1]

3. *A recognition and acceptance of the amount of personal power you have.* We recognize the influence we exert because of being in the helper position and having the status of a counselor. We do not dominate or misuse this power, but we

do feel confident and capable of ministering. If we have a need to be in control and/or to dominate, this is a misuse of our influence.

4. *The development of your own style of counseling.* Your style should be an expression of your own personality. You are open to learn from others and incorporate techniques and beliefs, but your style must be your own. Too often, counselors fall into the trap of simply parroting what they have read without sharpening and dissecting it and incorporating the information into their ministry.

5. *A willingness to be open, vulnerable, and a risk taker.* By the courage and risk taking you exhibit, you will encourage your counselees to do the same. We grow by being vulnerable, by trusting our intuitions at times, by identifying the feelings and struggles of others. We should admit our mistakes when we are wrong and should, when appropriate to do so, feel free to share with our counselees what we think and feel about them.

6. *A willingness to serve as a model for the person you are helping.* If we encourage people to take a risk, are we able to tell them the risks we have taken? If we encourage others to begin changing their lives through prayer, how will we respond when they ask us specifically how we have done this? Effective counselors do not ask their counselees to do things they are not willing to do. It is safe for us to sit in an office and dole out suggestions, advice, and guidelines for others. But the counselee has the right to inquire of us how we have done the same.

7. *A desire to grow and change.* I have had people say to me, "Norm, your thinking is different on this subject than a few years ago. This is not the same as you were teaching then." I reply, "I hope not. I want to keep changing and growing and learning. We never arrive." An example of this is my change from paying little attention fifteen years ago to the impact of the counselee's past upon his present. I still take, I hope, a balanced approach to this, but now I spend time identifying and working with the excess baggage of the past that is crippling the counselee's present. That is why I wrote *Making Peace with Your Past* and why I use many of

the principles in that book in my counseling practice. The past cannot be ignored. We need to be committed to a life of learning how to counsel more effectively.

8. *The ability to think on your feet.* You have neither the time nor the opportunity to ask the person to wait while you leave your office and go look up a response in some counseling book. Through years of study and prayer, you should be able to respond on a second's notice either through a statement, questions, or appropriate silence and then reflection.

9. *The ability to be a skilled listener.* Listening is putting into practice James 1:19: "Be a ready listener" and Proverbs 18:13, "If one gives answer before he hears, it is his folly and shame." A listener is one who is not thinking about what he or she is going to say when the other person stops talking. There is a difference between real versus pseudolistening. Being quiet when someone is talking does not constitute real listening. Listening is based on the intention to do one of four things: understand someone, enjoy someone, learn something, or give help or solace. Who are the people you listen to best? Who are those to whom you pseudolisten? We all have certain individuals who are difficult to listen to and whom we tune out. What makes it easy or hard for you to listen to others?

Let's consider some of the blocks to listening which may interfere with your helping another person.

If you are physically or emotionally exhausted, your listening ability will suffer. Have you ever counseled someone after a limited amount of sleep the night before? If so, you have probably had the experience, as I have, of feeling your eyelids gain ten pounds and the person in front of you begin to fade away. You may have tried pinching your thighs and shifting in your chair as sleep began to creep up on you. It's especially difficult if the counselee is speaking in a quiet monotone. Sometimes we fight against our humanity; what we need is a little more sleep.

Another listening roadblock is drawing premature conclusions. In your mind you have made a decision. *All right, I know what you're going to say,* you think to yourself. You may not say that aloud, but you finish the individual's story, and it may be a wrong conclusion. You may be reading into the person's words your own expectations, or projecting onto the other person what you would say or do in that situation.

Holding a bias or negative attitude toward certain individuals or even groups of people will affect your listening. These could include people who speak in a certain tone of voice, an ethnic group, the opposite sex, people who remind you of your past, or others. In effect you are saying, "If you are like . . . then I know what you are like and I don't want to listen to you." We all have our biases and this affects our listening.

Our outlook on life affects our listening also. If we have a strong sense of self-esteem our listening is different than if we are struggling with insecurity or self-condemnation. One person listens with optimism, another with pessimism. One hears the bad news, the other the good news.

Our own inner struggles may affect what we hear from another person. We have difficulty listening when our emotional involvement reaches the point where we are unable to separate ourselves from the other person.

Overload can be another roadblock in counseling. You may find that you have used up all the space you have for information and yet the counselee keeps feeding you more. There are times when I have to say, "You really have a lot happening in your life. Let me stop and see if I have caught what you want me to hear. I may need to jot a few of these down on paper to make sure that we can respond to all of them."

Remember that you have to work at listening. You can actually listen five times faster than another person talks, which gives a lot of time left over for your mind to wander.

Listen with your eyes as well as with your ears. Face-to-face messages are conveyed through the content, tone of voice, and nonverbals. But the nonverbals make up 55 percent of the message!

10. *Being more of an encourager than a confronter.* This characteristic of an effective counselor is my own bias. Let me explain what I mean, because both encouragement and confrontation are important and necessary. Too often those

in counseling have moved more toward confrontation because of the emphasis placed upon it in the past decade and because confrontation appears to be less time consuming and easier to use than thinking and feeling with the client. Let's look at both of these to understand their purpose.

Encouraging, along with listening, is one of the most important approaches you can take. To encourage means to urge forward, stimulating a person to do what he or she should be doing. Proverbs 12:25 says, "Anxiety in a man's heart weighs it down, but an encouraging word makes it glad" (*Amplified*). 1 Thessalonians 5:11 says, "Therefore encourage [admonish, exhort] one another and edify—strengthen and build up—one another, just as you are doing" (*Amplified*). To edify means to hold up or promote growth in Christian wisdom, grace, virtue, and holiness. Encouragement says to a person, "I believe in you as an individual, I believe you have the ability and the potential to follow through with this." Encouraging a person helps him to believe in his own personal worth, which is one of the goals of any type of counseling.

Confrontations are often used as a reflection of our own feelings of anger, frustration, impatience, or our desire to be in control. But confrontation can be used effectively when we are involved in helping another person. It is not an attack on the person "for his own good." Rather, it is an act in which the counselor points out to the person a discrepancy between his own and the counselee's manner of viewing reality. It is an extension of advanced empathy. How? It is based on a deep understanding of the counselee's feelings, experience, and behavior. It involves some unmasking of behavior and a challenge to action. Confrontations should only be used when empathy has been established.

The purpose of confronting is to help the person make better decisions for himself, to become more accepting of himself, and to be more productive and less destructive in his life. Sometimes we make a mistake by not confronting when it is necessary. We fear being wrong, misunderstood or rejected.

When then, should confrontation be used? A rule of thumb is, the stronger the relationship, the more powerful and intense the confrontation can be. It must occur because of your care and concern for the person. Do not use it too much during the early stages of counseling, because your relationship is not yet established. Ask yourself the question, "Can the person handle the confrontation at this time?" At the appropriate time, you can begin in a tentative manner with statements such as:

"I wonder if. . . ."

"Could it be . . . ?"

"Is it possible . . . ?"

"Does this make sense to you?"

"How do you react to this observation?"

11. *The ability to speak the other person's language.* One of my own personal goals in counseling during the first session is to discover the person's style of communication and communicate back to him or her in the same way. The principle is this: If I speak their language, real listening and change can occur. I try to discover whether the person is visually oriented, or more auditorially or kinesthetically (feeling) oriented. I listen to the tone of voice, volume, and the phrases he or she uses. I study the nonverbal communication. Some people are loud, expressive, and gesture a lot. Others are somewhat quiet, reserved, very proper and choose their words carefully. I join their style of communication which builds rapport, trust, and eventually, a willingness on their part to listen to me and follow my guidance.

This means the counselor will need to become very aware of his or her own style of communication. You will need to be flexible in order to use another style, and expand your vocabulary in order to make these shifts.

Several years ago, before I had read any material about this approach, I discovered its effectiveness with a couple of my clients. I was seeing a young couple from a traditional Italian family or "tribe" as they called themselves. They were outgoing, loud, and exuberant. They interrupted one another, outshouted one another, were full of enthusiasm and used a lot of gestures. In the first two sessions I got exactly nowhere with them. Instead of listening to me, they interrupted and ignored me. I was getting more and more frustrated. Before the third session with them I thought, *If you can't beat them, join them.* They weren't responding to *my* approach so I decided to communicate as they did.

When the session started I raised my voice along with theirs, interrupted them, and used their tone of voice and gestures. It worked wonderfully! They responded to me and we understood one another. I would lean forward, interrupt Tony, and say, "Tony! Tony! Listen to Maria. She's got something to say. Maria, tell him again." And my hands were gesturing for Tony to relax and listen to Maria. From then on we really worked well together.

After this third session, I left my office, which happened to be in my home, and went into the kitchen. My wife, who had been in the family room over sixty feet away, looked around the corner and asked, "Are you all right?"

"Yes, why?" I answered.

"I heard all this yelling and shouting in there," she said, "and wondered who was killing whom!"

"Nobody was killing anyone," I replied, "and no one was mad. That's the way those folks communicate." I found that I really looked forward to the sessions with them. And I enjoyed discovering that the counselor needs to adapt to the communication style of his or her counselees.

In marriage counseling I usually share with the couple that when they married, they each married a foreigner. I tell couples in premarital counseling that they are about to marry a foreigner. Needless to say, I receive some surprised reactions at times. But I hasten to say that the person to whom they are married or are about to marry comes from a different background, a different culture as it were, and has different values and beliefs. This person also speaks a different language whose words have different meanings. When each learns to speak the other person's language, then and only then will they be able to communicate and make significant contact with one another.

This concept makes sense to them. And so during our sessions I try to make them aware of one another's communication and language and begin to use it. This enables them to understand what they ordinarily would not understand. We don't use adult language and phrases with a small child who does not have the same experiences, vocabulary, and manner of reasoning we have. In a similar fashion, we can't expect other people to really understand us unless we move into their world.

To establish rapport in the first session of counseling you will need to meet people where they are. You must be perceptive to know if your communication is being accepted or rejected by the counselee. You can do this by reading the person's verbal and nonverbal language and his or her responses back to you. If you are communicating effectively, you don't have to make any adjustments. If not, you need the flexibility to change and do something different. If you would like the other person to change, you must change your own responses first. The counselee will usually change in response to the change he or she perceives in you. By becoming more flexible, you will have more influence and impact upon others. Here is another principle to consider: *In relationships, the person with the widest range of responses will have the greatest amount of influence and even control.*

THE IMPORTANCE OF PACING, AND SPEAKING STYLE

There are two important steps to follow in your counseling: one is pacing and the other is speaking the counselee's verbal language.

Pacing simply means meeting the other person where he or she is and matching his or her communication style. Pacing can mean picking up the mood, body language, and speech patterns which include tone of voice, volume, mood, and language. In a sense, pacing means responding to another person as though you were a mirror reflection of that person.

If you happen to be an "up" type of individual, friendly and chipper, and a counselee comes in very "down" and distressed, your mood may make the person feel you are not sensing what he or she is experiencing. I don't mean for you to act depressed, but to endeavor to match the volume, rate of speech, and tone to show that you are catching what that person is feeling.

I am an alert, ready-to-go person in the morning. Not everyone is. I remember one staff member with whom I worked for two years who was alert and energetic, but not at 9:00 in the morning. It took me awhile to realize that she could not handle an overload of information, presented with a lot of intensity and rapidity, first thing in the morning. I had to slow down and pace myself until she "came alive." Then it was all I could do sometimes to keep up with her! Sensitivity to your staff as well as your counselees will make your communication much more effective.

When you speak the other person's language, you are pacing. You are saying, "I'm with you," "I can be trusted," "I accept you."

Speaking the other person's language involves using words that are similar to that person's, and presenting them in a similar manner. Some individuals speak in short, brief sentences. Others give elaborate explanations. Listen to *how* the presentation is actually made and attempt to duplicate it. With couples, I have found that often one person gives two-line summaries, and the other a four-minute description. When I speak to the summarizer, in addition to using his language, I keep it very brief. And when I speak to the one who elaborates, I use more detail. (Usually I might add, it is the husband who summarizes and the wife who elaborates.)

I try to teach the couple that when the husband is speaking to his wife he should use her language and give more detail. And I suggest to the wife that when speaking to him she use his language and keep it very brief. This teaches them flexibility. Your task now is to custom design your own communication to reach those you counsel. If you work with a couple you become a translator.

As people grow and mature they develop their own ways of perceiving life. They take in or respond to life more through one of their response systems than the others. This is their way of processing information and making sense out of life. Some people are more *visually oriented;* they primarily use remembering and thinking. An *auditorially oriented* person is one who listens to life and depends upon spoken words for his information source. A *kinesthetically oriented* individual feels his way through his experiences. His feelings determine his responses. Of these three senses used by most people, one is preferred over the others.

For many years my dominant mode has been visual. I see life and respond to it more in that manner. If a secretary comes in and says, "Here's an interesting letter; let me read it to you," without thinking I usually say, "Oh, let me see it." I process it much faster and comprehend it better if I read it myself. If it is read to me, I might tend to "see" the sentences in my mind. Over the years, however, I have developed the auditory and the feeling modes as well out of necessity. Life has become fuller and more exciting for me by my being able to respond to the fullest with all of my senses. There are many situations in which we cannot respond with a visual mode and must use our auditory. Feelings also are very important.

I was raised as a typical male in our American culture. I had no male model of emotional expression, so for many years I was quite stunted emotionally. My retarded son Matthew was the instrument which God used to break open that part of my life and motivate me to feel. Through the many experiences with him over the past almost twenty years, I have felt the entire gamut of emotions in depth, including intense emotional frustration and pain. Yet, I wouldn't trade those experiences since I respond more fully to life, to others, and to God because of them. I can feel with and speak the language of the one who is kinesthetic.

How do you determine a person's dominate mode? It is very simple. Listen to the words he or she uses: their adjectives, verbs, predicates, and their descriptive language. They will tell you much through their words. Here are some visual phrases: "I *see* what you're saying." "That *looks* like a good idea." "*Show* me more about it." "It's kind of *hazy* at this time." "Let's get a new *perspective.*" "Let's shed some *light* on this." "Let's *focus* in on this." "What is your *point of view?*"

Here are some auditory examples: "That's as clear as a *bell.*" "This *sounds* good to me." "Can't you *tune* in to what I'm saying?" "*Tell* me that again." "That's coming through *loud* and *clear.*" "I *hear* you."

Here are some kinesthetic examples: "I have a good *feeling* about this." "I *sense* you're upset with me." "This day has a good *feel* to it." "Can you *grasp* what this means?" "That's a *heavy* problem." "Can you get *in touch* with that?"

Listen to what is said (that's auditory) and you will begin to see (that's visual) what they are sensing (that's kinesthetic) about their situation. Here are some illustrations to show what happens when we do not use the other person's language.

First Person: "If you would look over what I've written, you would see that I have really focused on the main issues. I don't see what the problem is." (Visual)

Second Person: "I get the feeling that something is missing. I am trying to sense what it is, but I'm still missing it." (Kinesthetic)

First Person: "Well, I think you're just locked into your point of view. Look at it from my perspective, will you?" (Visual)

Second Person: "I don't think you're in touch with the main problem." (Kinesthetic)

What are these two doing? They are talking past one another. Let's look at another miscommunication.

"I want to talk to you. I've got some ideas rattling about and I would like to know how they sound to you." (Auditory)

"Let's look at what you've got. Have you written them down for me?" (Visual)

"No. I'm just starting to tune into them myself. I guess I want to use you as a sounding board first. It's still not too clear even to me." (Auditory)

"Well, I'm pretty busy. When you have something to show me, then I can focus in and see what direction to go." (Visual)

Again there is miscommunication because neither person "sees" or "hears" the other's communication. But here is an example of clear communication. Notice the responses of the "Pacer."

"As I look over this paper you've written, I find some unclear areas in it. I am a bit fuzzy as to what you are trying to communicate." (Visual)

Pacing: "Yes. I think I see what you're getting at. Let me try to paint a picture of it for you and then we might see eye-to-eye on it."

"Look, I think we need to talk about this some more. I've listened to your concerns about the kids, but I'm not sure that we're on the same wave length." (Auditory)

Pacing: "Well, I think I can tune into what you're saying. Let's go back and do a replay of what we're saying and it will become clearer."

"I'm not in touch with what you're trying to communicate. I don't feel comfortable with this and I wonder about it. I don't sense the direction." (Kinesthetic)

Pacing: "I think I can feel your frustration. I would like to get a handle on this as well so we can both feel good about it."

Notice that in pacing there is communication. These concepts may be new to you, but they are the basis for relating to others effectively. Have you listened to your sermons or lessons? What type of words do you use? Which is your dominant mode? Remember that the congregation or class you minister to is made up of all three perceptual modes. You may want to rewrite some of your messages and experiment so that you speak the congregation's language. You might be surprised with the results.

Here is an illustration of how this approach is used in business. Below are three different descriptions of the same house. The real estate agent has described it in different ways depending upon the prospective buyer's perceptual mode. As you read these descriptions, which one appeals to you? It may tell you something about your dominant mode.

A: This house is quite picturesque. It has a very quaint look about it. You can see that a lot of focus has been put on the colorful patio and garden area. It has a lot of window space so that you can enjoy the view. It is clearly a good buy.

B: This house is very soundly constructed and situated. It is in such a quiet area that all you hear when you walk outside are the sounds of the birds singing. Its storybook interior has so much character you'll probably ask yourself how you could ever pass it by.

C: This house is not only solidly constructed, it has a real special feel to it as well. It's not often that you come in contact with a place that touches on so many features. It is spacious enough that you really feel you can move around freely, yet cozy enough that you won't wear yourself out taking care of it.[2]

Here are some words to help you learn this process.

VISUAL: focus, see, clear, bright, picture, perspective, show, hazy, colorful, pretty, peak, glimpse.

AUDITORY: listen, yell, talk, hear, harmony, noisy, discuss, call, loud, shout, told.

KINESTHETIC FEELING: feel, firm, touch, pressure, sense, concrete, hurt, touchy, irritated, clumsy, relaxed.

This approach to communication is taken from Neuro-Linguistic Programming (NLP) and can become very complicated. The original sources are cited at the conclusion of the chapter for those who would like to do in-depth study of this approach.

One other way to determine an individual's perceptual preference involves reading that person's eye movements. This is where the system can become a bit more complicated, but it is worth consideration. NLP suggests that a person's eyes can tell you much concerning his or her perception. The direction and position to which people briefly avert their eyes during the time they are recalling information or answering a question will correspond to their preferred way of responding. They break eye contact with you for a moment, and the eye movements can indicate whether they are using pictures, words, or feelings in their thinking or remembering process. These movements are called "assessing cues."

If they shift their eyes to the right and up, they are visualizing something they have never seen before. These are called *visual constructed images*. If they shift their eyes up and to the left, they are visualizing something they have seen before. These are called *visual remembered images*.

If they shift their eyes to the right but horizontal, they are hearing sounds or words never heard before. These are *auditory constructed* words and sounds. If the eye movement is horizontal, but to their left, the person is remembering sounds or conversations from the past. These are *auditory remembered* sounds or words.

If the individual looks to the right and down, he is sensing

34

inner, past feelings, or imagining future ones. If they look down and to the left, they are talking to themselves. These are *auditory sounds* or *words*. What kind of eye movements do *you* use? [3]

12. A final characteristic is *relying upon the Holy Spirit as your own personal counselor and your source of insight, guidance, and wisdom.* Dr. David Seamands defines a counselor as a temporary assistant to the Holy Spirit. We are temporary, because dependence upon us should never become permanent; and assistant, because our goal is to help others to be able to rely upon and relate directly with the Holy Spirit, our ultimate counselor.

These then are the characteristics of successful counselors. Counseling is a responsibility, a calling, an opportunity, and a ministry that has the potential of helping others change and mature. Our prayer is that we should be usable and effective change agents, led and guided by God. (For further study of the biblical guidelines to follow in counseling, see Proverbs 3:5, 6; 10:19; 11:13; 12:18; 16:24; 17:27; 21:23; 27:9; 29:20. The Amplified Bible is recommended.)

Now, the next major question is what do I actually do in counseling? What approach do I take? What works? What helps a person make life changes? The rest of this book is devoted to answering these questions. The integrated use of self-talk, imagery, and prayer may change your counseling ministry.

CHAPTER TWO

HAZARDS IN COUNSELING

EARLIER I STATED that the person doing the counseling is the most important ingredient in the counseling process. But it is important to identify those issues that can become hazards to the productivity of your counseling. As you read this chapter, please don't be thinking of how it might apply to *another* staff member or counselor. Take time to ask yourself some honest questions, to reflect, and to consider this as an opportunity for growth and change. The issues I am presenting are not limited to those in church ministry but can occur in any counseling environment whether you are a professional or a layperson.

Progress in counseling is hindered when we use the coun-

selee *to fulfill our personal needs.* This may be done uncon-
sciously or with full awareness. If there is a need to be powerful
or in control, we may tend to become too directive. This can
lead to the counselee's excessive dependence upon us. We
are not indispensable, but sometimes we feel as though we
are, and we may make statements that foster this type of
relationship.

If we have a strong need for approval and acceptance, we
may structure the counseling sessions in such a way that these
needs are reinforced. Many counselees want to please their
counselor or minister. Thus they may conform in order to
reinforce our need fulfillment. A question to consider: How
would you feel if the people you are counseling called and
said, "Thank you for the help you have given me. I feel as
though I am at a place where I can now handle life by myself.
I don't need to see you again?" What would your response
be to the person and to yourself? Your answer may say something about your own needs and the way you counsel.

Other questions to consider are: "How can you tell whether
you are counseling for the counselee's benefit or for your own?
How do you feel about your own sense of adequacy when
your counseling doesn't seem to be effective with a counselee?"

Counseling can be ineffective unless you have a clear understanding of what you are looking for in your sessions and what
you are seeking to accomplish. Before you read on, take a
few moments and list what it is you try to discover during
the first session. Then, turn to the conclusion of this chapter
and compare your list with the suggested list there. What
additional items did you suggest that I left out? How will
you go about discovering the answers to those questions which
have been listed for you?

GOALS IN COUNSELING

Let me suggest a few goals for the initial stages of counseling
and then the overall goal for any type of counseling. When
a person seeks you out, you are attempting to determine and
understand:

- the person's current situation
- how he or she has tried to handle the problem
- the counselee's perspective regarding the problem
- his or her reasons and motivation for coming to you for help
- the counselee's emotional reactions and his emotional strength

You are also attempting to:

- help the person clarify his or her life situation and how the problem relates to it, and
- see Christian growth occur through a new awareness of the application of Scripture and a vital prayer relationship.

Your main goal of counseling is to teach the process of problem-solving and to work yourself out of being needed. It is not sufficient to help them solve the specific problem that brings them to you. You must also teach them the process of problem-solving so that when other problems arise they will be equipped to handle them. When they learn this process, their need of you and me as counselors diminishes.

How can you tell whether you are helping the counselee learn to solve problems? How can you discover how the counselee perceives you and how you sound when you are counseling? You can't rely upon your own memory. Often we recall only what we want to remember—it's called selective remembrance.

If at all possible, and with the written permission of those you counsel, tape record some of your sessions. Then take time to listen and evaluate yourself. Videotaping is even better because it allows you to observe your facial expressions and mannerisms as well as the words you say. By monitoring your counseling in this way you can discover what you do, why you do it, and the effect it has on the counselee. Here are some important questions to use when reviewing your sessions.

1. How many questions do you ask? If they are numerous, are they to obtain information or to assist the counselee to think and grow? Do you ask questions because you don't know what else to do or to keep the sessions moving?

2. Do you give advice and tend to work quickly toward solutions? Or is there an emphasis upon sharing and exploring feelings in depth?

3. Who gives direction to the sessions? You or the counselee? Who structures what you do?

4. How do you pray for the session prior to seeing the individual? What is the purpose of your prayer during the session? Is this something *you* want to do or the counselee?

5. How much support and reassurance do you offer? Do you give it before the person has the opportunity to fully share his or her feelings and experiences? Is there anything you might be doing that hinders them from sharing their feelings?

6. Do you confront the counselees when it is needed or do you hesitate? Do your comments assist them in thinking deeper about their situation?

7. Who does most of the talking? What percentage of the time are you talking and what percentage does the counselee? Do you hear yourself preaching, pushing, or persuading?

8. Can you find an indication that you are responsive to what the counselee is saying?

9. How often do you reflect back to the person what you heard him or her saying? If you do this, what is the purpose?

10. How much do you interpret or suggest a different meaning to what a person has shared? Do you *tell* them or *assist* them by guiding them to discover this for themselves?

11. Do you go into counseling with a well-defined plan or wait to see what is shared by the individual?

12. Do you rigidly follow a certain style of counseling in your session, or are you flexible and do you adapt to the person?

13. Are you comfortable with the techniques you use or are they "too borrowed"? Is your approach mechanical or have you made it your own?

14. How do your counselees respond to your approach? Is it positive or negative? [1]

Another major hazard that interferes with counseling is the presence of *unresolved conflicts* within our own lives. I am not suggesting that we wait to help others until we are free of stress, tension, and problems ourselves. But we must be aware of our own biases and those areas of our own lives we would rather not face. The issue is not *whether* you are struggling with a problem, but *how* you are struggling. If you are aware of your own contribution to the difficulty and your alternatives for resolution, your counseling will probably not be affected.

What happens if you are experiencing despair and hopelessness and at the same time are trying to work with those in a similar situation? What happens if you still have intense anger toward a dominant mother and your counselee is a dominant, controlling woman? Some of us have hurts from the past which are like abscesses or wounds that have been covered by scabs. If the issue brought to us by a person in need is similar, our scab may begin to come off revealing a still bleeding wound. When we have resolved the issue from the past and scar tissue replaces the bleeding wound, our experience can be used to assist others.

Scripture admonishes us to let Christ live in and through us, to put on the new man and allow old things to pass away (Galatians 4:19; Ephesians 4:23, 24; 2 Corinthians 5:17). This is our goal for those we counsel. But it must be the goal for our own lives as well. In order to help others break free from the influence of their past, we need to have accomplished that step or be in the process of completing it. May I suggest that you read my book *Making Peace With Your Past* for two reasons: to be able to recommend it at the appropriate time for your counselees and to assist you in looking at any possible hindrances to your own counseling ministry.

Another hazard is the presence of *personal insecurities, fears, beliefs and expectations about yourself and your counseling.* You may be concerned about your own ability to counsel. You may wonder whether you have any giftedness in this field but feel that you must counsel especially if you are a minister. You will feel the gap between what you know and what you are called upon to do in counseling. We all do to some degree! I am not sure that our concerns about our ability are ever completely resolved.

Listed below are some typical concerns of those involved in counseling. I would like you to read through them and identify those which you relate to at this time. Once you have done that ask yourself, "Why do I feel this way? Why do I believe this? Is this a legitimate concern or expectation?" In a sense, I am asking you to begin to look at your own beliefs and self-talk which is a major portion of what this book is all about. Practice what you will be asking your counselees to do as you work with them.

I'm afraid that I will make some mistakes in counseling.
My counselees will suffer because of my lack of ability and knowledge.
I'm not sure what to do in serious crisis situations.
I must be perfect in my counseling and feel I should know more all the time.
Silence really threatens me in counseling.
I need to know that my counselees are improving.
I have difficulty with demanding, dominant counselees.
I have negative feelings toward those who are poorly motivated.
I have difficulty deciding the direction to take in counseling sessions.
I should be successful in ministering to every person I see.
I feel uptight and on the spot when I counsel.
I have difficulty expressing feelings of anger with a counselee.
I wonder how honest to be with the counselee.
I wonder how much of my personal life to reveal in counseling.
I sometimes wonder if I am doing what's best and really helping the person.
I worry about my own feelings toward some of the people I counsel.
I sometimes daydream when counseling others.

I struggle with knowing whether to give advice or not.
I have concerns about counseling others whose values are different from mine.[2]

Did you identify with any of these? Are your concerns valid or is there too much concern? You may want to discuss your responses with other counselors. You will find that they have similar concerns, but you may get some help from them as well.

One of the hazards of counseling on the part of both the counselor and the counselee is the desire for instant relief and help. Our society reflects this mentality of instant results. It is difficult for adults and children alike to wait for their rewards. We have instant photos, instant food, instant tea, etc. With this attitude a helper may assume his or her role is to solve all problems that are brought to counseling. However, counselees do not usually make immediate change or progress. Please remember that! There may be some symptoms of relief, but at the same time their anxiety and even their problems may initially increase. The counselees are looking at life in a closer and different manner. By coming to you for help they are beginning to relinquish some of their defenses. They are admitting they cannot handle what is taking place. The anxiety associated with their vulnerability is a reflection of their discomfort.

Much of the success of your counseling will be the result of listening and giving the person your undivided attention. If you are in a hurry, or even appear to be hurried, the hurting person feels rejected and may pull back from being open and honest. If you look for immediate results, you will probably make decisions and build conclusions that are inaccurate. There will be a tendency to read things into what the counselee is saying or even finish his sentences or stories with your own endings. Relaxed and attentive listening supports the person and helps you capture what he or she is really trying to convey to you.

As a counselor, you cannot measure your success by how soon the person leaves counseling, by how many marriages stay together, or by how often the counselee tells you he or she is being helped. As in so many other areas of ministry and of the Christian walk, we are called to be faithful. You may not see the results of your counseling until months later. To be lasting and genuine, growth and progress need to be slow.

Another hazard in counseling is the belief that *we can work with every person who comes to us for help.* That would be nice, but there are some personalities, some problems that are too uncomfortable and some which are too serious for us to ever attempt to handle. Even experienced professionals have to discern which clients they can assist and which need to be referred to someone with greater skill or ability to relate to that problem. You cannot work with all clients. You need a good referral source so that you may call on specialists. It is all right to admit that you cannot help everyone, yet some in ministry have difficulty doing that. There are many reasons for this, but what is most important is to identify what type of cases or counselees would fall in your own "difficult to counsel" perspective.

Being judgmental is not our calling in the counseling office. Not only is it important for us to be nonjudgmental but we must also listen nonjudgmentally. If a counselee has to hide his or her feelings and behaviors from you, growth will not occur. This individual needs the freedom to speak openly in his or her own language.

One of the ways in which I teach my classes at Talbot Theological Seminary is by doing live demonstrations in front of the class. I do this for both premarital and marital counseling classes. The couples or individuals who agree to counsel in this way are very aware of and comfortable with the fact that there may be forty to seventy individuals observing the counseling process.

One year, a pastor who was enrolled in the class knew that I was looking for a married couple and said he had a young couple in need of counseling. They agreed to come and be counseled in this manner. The couple had been believers for three months. He was a piano mover with biceps the size of my thighs. He was in AA and had been arrested the year before for breaking up a bar. As we started the process of counseling, the man and his wife were polite and a bit reserved.

After a few minutes the wife asked, "Can we talk here as we usually talk?"

"Yes, of course," I replied.

The air turned blue! Their language came alive and they argued, attacked and swore! The students were in shock. During that first session, the wife's biggest gripe was the fact that just recently they had taken a trip to Tijuana, Mexico, with some friends and he had tried to sell her in a topless bar! The second session was a disaster because the husband came in loaded on pot and alcohol. During the third session of counseling in front of this class, the issue we worked on was his fear of praying out loud with his wife. It was an amazing view of life as it is in the real world. I couldn't have asked for a better couple for students. They had a preview of what the ministry is really like!

It would have been easy to sit in judgment of this couple, but the counseling office is not the place. When we are judgmental, we actually attack the person's sense of worth. We are saying that the person is bad or good instead of evaluating what the person is doing and the impact of those actions on the problem situation.

If your counselees sense that you are sitting in judgment of them, they will erect defenses or attempt to please you as though you were a parent. Your acceptance of them gives them a realm of security from which they can view their situation more objectively. If you judge, they may attempt to convince you that they have resolved their difficulty or they may give up trying.

It is very easy to carry a ministerial teaching and preaching role over into the counseling office. But counseling is not telling people what they are doing wrong, what to do right, and why they should do it.

Finally, I just mention the *problem of leakage.* This is another word for the breaking of confidentiality. One of the unique difficulties ministers have, compared to the professional counselor, is the combination of preaching/teaching and counseling. The preacher looks for fresh illustrations from life situations. But using a recent counseling experience for the Sunday morning message, with the counselee sitting in the congregation, can have devastating results. The illustration may make a point and create a greater interest for some, but it may also stop people from seeking future counsel. They don't want to end up as the Sunday morning example.

When ministers get together, they often engage in swapping counseling experiences and stories that are unique and even shocking. This may violate the confidentiality of the counseling relationship. In most states a minister has privileged communication and confidentiality. What is shared in counseling, needs to stay with us and us alone. It is not to be shared with your spouse. He or she does not have a need to know.

At a ministers' conference I was discussing this matter and a pastor's wife came up and asked why her husband shouldn't share his counseling experiences and who he saw with her. I replied, "I hope you aren't offended by this, but very frankly, it is really none of your business. You don't have a need to know." Fortunately, she responded well, but my statement was the bottom line.

We must be seen as trustworthy individuals and hold what is shared with us as a sacred trust before God. Proverbs 11:13 states, "He who goes about as a talebearer reveals secrets, but he who is trustworthy and faithful in spirit keeps the matter hidden" (*Amplified*). And Proverbs 20:19 says, "He who goes about as a talebearer reveals secrets; therefore associate not with him who talks too freely" (*Amplified*).

CONFIDENTIALITY AND PRIVILEGED COMMUNICATION

Laws concerning confidentiality and privileged information vary from state to state for ministers, and even for professional counselors. Most of the time what is revealed to you is privileged information and is to be held in confidence. But there are a few exceptions. It is important that you check with a lawyer or state agency to determine the laws for your state and learn when you must inform the authorities because of a difficulty. In some states some of the courts have determined that if an individual intends to take harmful, dangerous, or criminal action against another human being, or against himself, it is the counselor's duty to warn appropriate individuals of such intentions. Those warned may include a variety of persons such as:

1. the person or the family of the person who is likely to suffer the results of harmful behavior
2. the family of the client who intends to harm himself or someone else
3. associates or friends of those threatened or making threats
4. law enforcement officials

Your state laws may also require notification of law enforcement or public health agencies in situations where indications of suicide, child abuse, or sexual abuse are present.

In the state of California, there are very specific laws concerning child abuse and sexual abuse. These apply to a large number of those involved with children including teachers, principals, day-care workers, foster parents, medical doctors, dentists, psychologists, marriage and family therapists, religious practitioners, and many others. (Religious practitioner means those ministers recognized by their denomination, organization, or religion.)

The law states that any of these people who, in their professional capacity or within the scope of their employment, reasonably suspect that a child has been the victim of abuse shall report the known or suspected instance to a child protective agency immediately or as soon as is practically possible by telephone. He or she will then prepare and send a written report within thirty-six hours after learning of the incident. And no person who makes such a report shall be civilly or criminally liable for any report required by the stated laws. If a person fails to report an instance of child abuse, as specified by law, he or she will be guilty of a misdemeanor.

Ask an authority to go over your state laws with you to explain them and their interpretation.

Identifying and confronting the hazards of counseling will help you produce greater results in your counseling ministry. Your counseling problems will diminish as you place yourself in the role of the counselee. By allowing yourself to be counseled and directed by God through the ministry of the Holy Spirit, your ability, sensitivity, and inner security will develop and become more usable for others.

QUESTIONS TO ASK YOURSELF IN COUNSELING

As you counsel a person in a scheduled counseling session, consider these questions.

1. *What kind of person does the counselee seem to be?* How did the person respond to you? How did he or she begin the interview? What were the person's beginning words in the interview? What seemed to be the counselee's feelings at this point?

2. *Did this person have some motivation for coming for counseling* or was it suggested by someone else? Will he or she probably have enough motivation to make use of counseling?

3. *What precipitated the counselee's coming to see you at this time?* Usually some culmination of events has brought the person to seek help.

4. *Has the person made previous efforts to obtain help for his or her problems?* If so, what were the circumstances and what was the outcome?

5. *How has the counselee hoped or expected counseling would be of benefit?*

6. *What does he or she see as the problems?* How are the problems presented? Are they of recent origin or longstanding? When did the counselee recognize that he or she had the problems?

7. *Is the counselee currently under medical treatment?* Does the doctor know about his or her coming for counseling? If not, is he or she willing for the counselor to be referred to a physician if necessary? Note any significant health, economic, social, or cultural factors.

8. *If the counselee is married, was there a desire to obtain marriage counseling with the spouse?* Does the spouse wish to see someone too? If the counselee wishes the counselor to see the spouse, what is his expectation or hope? Are parents or families of either of the marriage partners involved in the problem? What is the attitude of these persons toward the marriage or proposed marriage?

9. At the close of the first interview, *carefully evaluate your impression of the person and the situation.* In particular you should note:

a. Whether the person has been able to delineate the problems so that he or she has defined the areas where help is needed.

b. How has the counselee reacted and how is he or she now reacting to his situation? Do these reactions appear to be appropriate to the real situation?

c. What is your evaluation of the person's strengths? Is he or she going to be able to make good use of the counseling?

CHAPTER THREE

THOUGHT LIFE—THE FOUNDATION FOR COUNSELING

SHE'S SITTING THERE IN THE PEW next to her family, an interested expression on her face. Her facial muscles move from time to time and her eyes shift now and then. She gives all the appearance of being involved in the proceedings of the morning service. When she walked in with her husband and two children, she was open, friendly, and even animated. Forty minutes later she seems quite involved in the worship service. But is she? What would we hear if we could tap into her thought life as the police often put a tap on a suspect's phone and office? What you hear could be totally foreign to what you anticipate.

Listen with me for a moment as we eavesdrop on this wom-

51

an's self-talk. *Oh, I should never have come this morning. I just know that Jack is upset with me again. Nothing, absolutely nothing has gone right lately. I wish this depression would go away. I just know something is wrong, the way Jack's been acting. I wonder if other people can tell how I feel. Why did the pastor choose today to preach on that subject? Doesn't he know what that does to me?* Her thoughts continue in that vein for the remainder of the service. As she walks out, once again she gives all the appearance of being a satisfied, happy person. But we know differently, don't we?

A high school boy sits in the front row looking very intent throughout the service. He must be agreeing with most of what was shared during the hour because he nods in a positive way from time to time. He is smartly dressed and seems to be popular with his peers. He is sought after by several colleges for both his academic and athletic abilities. He seems to have his life together and there is a bright future ahead of him. Once again let's tap into his thought life during the church service. *I really feel numb. . . . I wonder what the church people will say about me. . . . I guess I don't really care. I don't care about anything. I don't know why I'm this way . . . huh?—I wonder what the pastor said this morning. I haven't heard a word so far. This is the only way to go. . . . I'm never going to be different. I know that others suspect me. They must be talking about me. Well . . . hmm—this will give them something to talk about. Two hours to go . . . two hours to live.*

You would never know the inner thoughts, the inner feelings, the inner turmoil of either of these two people from an outward glance. Only God knows the inward feelings and thoughts of the mind. Yet our thought life causes us the most problems. It is the thought life of the counselee that is the foundation of our counseling.

If you are a pastor, think of this. As you sit on the platform, waiting for your church service to begin, what goes through *your* mind? What type of thoughts are churning around, or are you aware of them? You *do* talk to yourself, you know. That's very normal. And if you're a pastor, I hope you realize that the people sitting there as a congregation are talking to themselves as well. In fact, many are holding inner conversations with themselves while you're preaching.

We all carry on conversations with ourselves daily. But are you aware of the importance and impact of this? Self-talk *initiates* and *intensifies* our *emotions.* Self-talk directs the way in which we *behave* toward others. Self-talk determines what we *say* to others. Keep this thought in mind as we begin to discover what we are going to do in counseling and why we will be doing it.

The struggle and desire to develop a biblical system of counseling has been coming to the forefront more in the past several years than ever before. Some ministers and counselors have attempted to develop their model of counseling by superimposing a psychological theory of counseling upon biblical teaching. In some instances there appears to be a correlation. But in others the biblical teaching is distorted as they attempt to mold it to fit their preconceived ideas. The other approach is to begin with a biblical perspective and use it to screen psychological theories of counseling.

Various attempts at reconciling the two will probably continue for several years. Perhaps there never will be an absolute standard of counseling reflecting integration between psychological theories and biblical teaching. In the meantime, however, it is possible to find indications from the Scriptures concerning how to minister to others.

THE BASICS FOR COUNSELING

The starting place for developing a method of counseling or helping others is not the consideration of specific techniques, but rather, a focus upon the nature of God and the nature of man. What we believe about God—who he is, his attributes, and what he desires for mankind—certainly influences how we respond to the people with whom we have contact and to whom we have been called upon to minister. How we view man—who he is, his potentials, and his defects—certainly influences how we respond to individuals within the context of counseling. A.W. Tozer said that a right conception of God is basic not only to systematic theology but to practical Christian living as well.

As we look at who man is, several facts must be remembered. Man was created by God and was made in the image of God, but because of the Fall, a distortion has occurred in the image of God within man. Man is a sinful being, yet he is very, very worthwhile and worth redeeming. A counselor who sees man as being totally good with no problems or defects will respond to individuals in counseling in a manner reflecting that belief. Another counselor may see man as totally lost, totally deficient, with no good or worth or potential within him whatsoever, and will respond in a different manner. But if we see the individual as made in the image of God, yet sinful but with potential, perhaps the balance we are seeking in our counseling can be found.

As we approach man in counseling, we need to consider man's need. What *is* his basic need? One suggestion is that man needs to regard himself as a worthwhile human being. This has nothing to do with *feeling* worthwhile; it is an examination of the evidence, the realization and the conclusion that we are worthwhile regardless of our feelings. Knowing who God is and who man is affects counseling. There are several goals of counseling, some of which depend upon the status of the counselee.

For those who have never entered into a relationship with Jesus Christ, new birth is definitely a goal. Another goal, for those who have not yet been born again and for those who have been Christians for some time, is a greater understanding of who God is. For such persons, a teaching ministry concerning the attributes of God would be an appropriate recommendation. For one who is already a Christian, Christlikeness, as expressed in Ephesians 4:13, is a suitable goal.

Because the self-concept is at the heart of so many difficulties, helping a counselee develop a positive self-concept is a major objective. This is accomplished through an understanding of the extent of God's acceptance, which leads to one's own acceptance and a healthy self-concept.

Worthiness, competence, and a sense of belonging are important factors in the development of a healthy self-concept. In a relationship with God the Father, a person is assured of belongingness. This is seen in passages such as Matt. 6:9;

Eph. 1:6; John 3:16; and Rom. 8:15–17. As Maurice Wagner says,

> He is pleased to call us His son. This gives us a position
> with Him in His family. We know we are somebody to
> God. We have been redeemed from being a nobody. The
> idea of being a nobody never again will have any validity.
> When it threatens us we can firmly reject it in the reas-
> surance of God's promise.[1]

In our relationship with Jesus, the Son of God, we are assured
of worthiness (John 3:36; 2 Cor. 5:18; 1 John 1:9). Dr. Wagner
also says that we gain a secure sense of competence as we
relate to the Holy Spirit, who is the Comforter, the Guide,
and the source of great strength. The Holy Spirit directs a
person's attention to Christ. "He shall testify of me," says John
15:26. We see this also in John 14:26. The Holy Spirit imparts
the love of God (Rom. 5:5), imparts hope (Rom. 15:13), and
gives joy (Rom. 14:17; Gal. 5:22; 1 Thess. 1:6).

So many people who come for counseling focus their attention on their incompetence and unworthiness, and upon their
distortions. The minister's role is to encourage and help counselees see themselves as being in the image of God instead
of focusing upon the distortions in this image. As Lloyd Ahlem
expresses it in his book *Do I Have To Be Me?*

> The writers of the Scriptures are careful to point out that
> when God looks at you in Jesus Christ, He sees you as a
> brother to His own Son. Because of the work of Christ,
> all the ugliness of humanity is set aside. God has absolutely
> no attitude of condemnation toward man. You are worth
> all of God's attention. If you were the only person in
> the whole world, it would be worth God's effort to make
> Himself known to you and to love you. He gives you freely
> the status and adequacy of an heir to the universe.[2]

We need to help our counselees realize that God also knows
who we are and loves us in spite of our feelings of inadequacy.
J. I. Packer, in his book *Knowing God* put it better than anyone else:

What matters supremely, therefore, is not, in the last analysis, the fact that I know God, but the larger fact which underlies it—the fact that *He knows me*. I am graven in the palms of His hands. I am never out of His mind. All my knowledge of Him depends on His sustained initiative in knowing me. I know Him, because He first knew me, and continues to know me. He knows me as a friend, one who loves me; and there is no moment when His eye is off me, or His attention distracted from me, and no moment, therefore, when His care falters.

This is momentous knowledge. There is unspeakable comfort—the sort of comfort that energizes, be it said, not enervates—in knowing that God is constantly taking knowledge of me in love, and watching over me for my good. There is tremendous relief in knowing that His love to me is utterly realistic, based at every point on prior knowledge of the worst about me, so that no discovery now can disillusion Him about me, in the way I am so often disillusioned about myself, and quench His determination to bless me. There is, certainly, great cause for humility in the thought that He sees all the twisted things about me that my fellow-men do not see (and am I glad!), and that he sees more corruption in me than that which I see in myself (which, in all conscience, is enough). There is, however, equally great incentive to worship and love God in the thought that for some unfathomable reason, He wants me as His friend, and desires to be my friend, and has given His Son to die for me in order to realise this purpose.[3]

In counseling, what approach should a minister take to achieve these goals? Not only must the question of technique be considered, but as we look at the counselee's life, we must also decide what area of the person's life to concentrate upon. Do we deal just with his or her thoughts? Do we deal only with behavior? Do we deal just with feelings? Is there an area that should be ignored, left out, or even played down?

In any counseling approach or system one rarely finds an emphasis on all three of these. Some, such as Reality Therapy, emphasize behavior. Rational Emotive Therapy or Cognitive Therapy deal specifically with thought process. The nondirective or client-centered approach deals basically with the feelings of the person and makes little attempt to analyze his or her thoughts or behavior. The Scripture itself speaks of all three—feelings, thoughts, and behavior.

In the life and ministry of Jesus we see occasions on which he was sensitive to the feelings of others. At other times he emphasized rational thinking. On still other occasions he focused on behavior. It appears that the Scriptures specifically talk more about behavior and thinking, however, than about feelings.

Some passages in the Scriptures that emphasize the thinking process or the thought process are Genesis 6:5; 8:21; 1 Chronicles 28:9; Proverbs 15:15; 16:2; 23:7; Isaiah 26:3; Romans 8:6, 7; 12:2; Ephesians 4:23; and 1 Peter 1:13.

There is a strong interrelationship between thoughts, feelings, and behavior. Most of our emotions or feeling responses come from our thought life; what we dwell upon, what we think about, can stimulate feelings. The words *think, thought,* and *mind* are used over three hundred times in the Scriptures. Often, a person's behavior can influence both feelings and thoughts. Then, once a person has certain feelings, those feelings can intensify or reinforce a particular thinking pattern and can also influence one's behavior.[4]

Let's look further at the influence of our thoughts. All of us begin to learn from early childhood to formulate thoughts, perceptions, and feelings in words, phrases, and sentences. Most of us, by the time we become adults, regulate most of our important thinking and consequently our emotions in terms of our internalized sentences or self-talk. The basic principle and premise for this book and for our counseling is this: WHAT PEOPLE SAY TO THEMSELVES GOVERNS THE WAY THEY FEEL AND ACT!

Even emotions, such as anxiety, anger, love, or elation are often associated with or result from self-talk. Each emotion is determined by the kind of self-talk expressed. Disturbed behaviors and excessive emotional responses which you will see in those you counsel can stem from what has occurred in the mind. This does not mean that each behavior or emotion is preceded by a series of statements. Many of our responses have become automatic. Negative thoughts, self-defeating thoughts, and anxiety creating statements become as automatic and unconscious as driving a car. Part of our goal in ministry is to assist others in becoming aware of such thoughts.

Charles Swindoll describes the importance of thoughts in this way:

Thoughts, positive or negative, grow stronger when fertilized with constant repetition. That may explain why so many who are gloomy and gray stay in that mood, and why others who are cheery and enthusiastic continue to be so, even in the midst of difficult circumstances. Please do not misunderstand. Happiness (like winning) is a matter of right thinking, not intelligence, age, or position. Our performance is directly related to the thoughts we deposit in our memory bank. We can only draw on what we deposit.

What kind of performance would your car deliver if every morning before you left for work you scooped up a handful of dirt and put it in your crankcase? The fine-tuned engine would soon be coughing and sputtering. Ultimately, it would refuse to start. The same is true of your life. Thoughts about yourself and attitudes toward others that are narrow, destructive, and abrasive produce wear and tear on your mental motor. They send you off the road while others drive past.[5]

Any counseling approach must help counselees become aware of their self-talk, identify it, become aware of its effect and make the appropriate changes. This sounds simple, doesn't it! But it takes great effort and consistency since counselors will be working against years of training and reinforcement. We will discuss that later.

The biblical basis for an emphasis upon the counselee's thinking process and thought life is found throughout the

Word of God. "As [a man] thinketh in his heart, so is he" (Prov. 23:7 KJV) is at the heart of our relationale. We also find that "the thoughts of the righteous are right, but the counsels of the wicked are deceit" (Prov. 12:5 KJV); "for they that are after the flesh do mind the things of the flesh; but they that are after the Spirit, the things of the Spirit (Rom. 8:5 KJV). The word *mind,* from the Greek *phroneo* means "to think." The Word of God teaches that what we think is a reflection of either our old nature or our new nature. If this is so, it is vital that we give close attention to the type of self-talk we are using.

In this type of counseling, we encourage the individual to engage in self-observation, to become sensitive to what he or she is saying inwardly. Scripture teaches this. "Search me, O God, and know my heart! Try me and know my thoughts! And see if there be any wicked way in me, and lead me in the way everlasting!" (Ps. 139:23, 24). How is this done? Again, through the Scripture. "For the word of God is living and active, sharper than any two-edged sword, piercing to the division of soul and spirit, of joints and marrow, and discerning the thoughts and intentions of the heart" (Heb. 4:12).

Scripture states that the heart is the center of our intellectual and volitional life. The Bible also teaches that the thoughts of our hearts need to be considered. Jesus said, " 'What comes out of a man is what defiles a man . . . All these evil things come from within, and defile a man" (Mark 7:20, 23). (Other passages include Matthew 9:4; 15:19; Luke 2:19, 51; 5:22; 9:47; 24:38.) We are aware of some of our thoughts and others go unnoticed. But you and I can become aware of our thoughts and we need to develop the ability to become an accurate observer of them. The Scripture tells us to bring "into captivity every thought to the obedience of Christ" (2 Cor. 10:5 KJV). Our thought life is so basic and important that God created us so that feelings are to follow our thoughts. Many people today, however, have reversed the process and in so doing live a life of instability. Thoughts and feelings need to be considered in their proper order.

In Philippians, Paul shows us the connection between our thoughts and feelings:

Have no anxiety about anything, but in everything by prayer and supplication with thanksgiving let your requests be made known to God. And the peace of God, which passes all understanding, will keep your hearts and your minds in Christ Jesus.

Finally, brethren, whatever is true, whatever is honorable, whatever is just, whatever is pure, whatever is lovely, whatever is gracious, if there is any excellence, if there is anything worthy of praise, think about these things. What you have learned and received and heard and seen in me, do; and the God of peace will be with you. . . .

Not that I complain of want; for I have learned, in whatever state I am, to be content. . . . I can do all things in him who strengthens me. (Phil. 4:6–9, 11, 13)

We need to remember that the power of this passage is made possible through a personal relationship with Jesus Christ. This is how the reality of peace in our lives is finally realized. In this passage, Paul is stating that what is said must be practiced; this means repeated again and again and again. It is important that a person's new thoughts initiate a new series of behaviors. These behaviors must be incompatible with old behaviors if change is to be lasting and generalized.

Counseling must be closely tied to theology and biblical truth. God's purpose for all of us is to conform us to the image of his Son. Colossians 3:10 states, "being renewed unto knowledge after the image of him that created him." This renewal is a continuing process through sanctification, which allows us to become what we were created to be; and it is related to our self-talk. As we are being renewed, our self-talk becomes more Christlike and less and less of the "old man."

Thoughts play a vital role in the sanctification process. From the pen of Paul, we see this in Ephesians 4:22–25:

Put off your old nature which belongs to your former manner of life and is corrupt through deceitful lusts, and be renewed in the spirit of your minds, and put on the new nature, created after the likeness of God in true righteousness and holiness. Therefore, putting away falsehood, let every one speak the truth with his neighbor, for we are members of one another.

The renewal here is the spirit of the mind. Under the controlling power of the Holy Spirit, a believer directs his thoughts and energies toward God. "Do not be conformed to this world but be transformed by the renewal of your mind, that you may prove what is the will of God, what is good and acceptable and perfect" (Rom. 12:2). The renewing of the mind is the adjustment of the person's thinking and outlook on life so that these conform to the mind of God.

In counseling we need to direct counselees to focus their thoughts on Christlike thoughts. "If then you have been raised with Christ, seek the things that are above, where Christ is, seated at the right hand of God. Set your minds on things that are above, not on things that are on earth" (Col. 3:1, 2). "Set your affections on" is to think on, or focus on. Ephesians 1:18 says, "having the eyes of our heart enlightened," or "having the eyes of your heart flooded with light" (as the Amplified has it).

The heart is the core or center of the person's inmost self. Feelings, words, and actions stem from it. These enlightened eyes come through the work and power of the Holy Spirit. The power that a believer has available to him or her is the same power that God used to raise Christ from the dead! And as this then translates to our mind or thought life, we need to assist those whom we help to realize that God through his power gives each person the ability to picture things in the way he pictures them. We all need a transformation of the mind, to have the mind of Christ. Lloyd Ogilvie, pastor of the First Presbyterian Church of Hollywood, has said that "each of us needs to surrender the kingdom of our mind to God." As you work with each person in counseling, ask yourself, "Has this person surrendered his or her mind to be a resting place for the Spirit of God?" If not, the goal of your counseling then becomes quite clear.

This new type of thinking is not to be a mechanical or rote process void of personal involvement and a desire to change. These new thoughts need to become personalized responses with meaning.

One of the goals of this approach to counseling is to use Scripture in an effective manner to help counselees properly view their situations and develop change-producing thought patterns. The basis for the role of biblical truth in the change process is seen in the following passages.

"All Scripture is inspired by God and profitable for teaching, for reproof, for correction, and for training in righteousness, that the man of God may be complete, equipped for every good work" (2 Tim. 3:16, 17).

"For the Word of God is living and active, sharper than any two-edged sword, piercing to the division of soul and spirit, of joints and marrow, and discerning the thoughts and intentions of the heart" (Heb. 4:12).

"I will observe thy statutes; O forsake me not utterly! How can a young man keep his way pure? By guarding it according to thy word" (Ps. 119:8, 9).

Part of your task in counseling is to help the individual first to see the real value of the specific Scripture and then to incorporate and integrate the passage into his or her life. Involved in this process of restructuring the thought process is the use of prayer and imagery. Without making rash claims, the integrative use of these three approaches—Scripture, prayer, and imagery—become a significant step in the change process.

CHAPTER FOUR

THE INNER CONVERSATION APPROACH TO COUNSELING

YOU ARE SITTING IN YOUR OFFICE looking at the distraught individual across from you. For the past ten minutes he has been telling you about his inner turmoil. As the story unfolds, you can feel his distress and also see why the problem is continuing. You realize there is very little you can suggest or do to change the actual difficulty. What you can do is help him with his thinking about the situation. You are just about ready to begin—but wait!

Do you *really* know what to say to this person? Do you know *what* to do in a practical specific manner to help this person with his thought life? Do you know how to *combine* the use of new self-talk, imagery, and prayer in order to bring about the best results? Do you know *why* you are doing what you are about to do? Understanding the basic principles and premises for your counseling is extremely important before you proceed.

"Cognitive counseling" or "therapy" is the correct term for this approach in psychological circles. I prefer the term "inner conversation" because it is simple and the average person can relate to it. Let's look at the basic principles upon which the inner conversation approach is based.

THOUGHTS CREATE EMOTIONAL DISORDERS

The inner conversation approach is based on the belief that thoughts can create emotional disorders. Many common psychological disorders occur because of distortions and aberrations in thinking. Thus in your counseling you will be suggesting effective techniques to help a person overcome his distortions, blindspots, and self-deceptions. Very simply, your goal will be to lead the person to a pattern of thinking that will reflect the teaching of Scripture. Both the problem in a person's life and the remedy are found in the thinking process.

Because we are emphasizing thinking, it does not mean that the immediate source of stress, the emotional reactions, are being deemphasized. It simply means that we are seeking to minister to the emotional responses through the thinking function. By changing errors of thought and perception, stability can come to the emotional side of a person's life. Correcting the person's thought life consists of helping him or her become aware of thinking, identifying what thoughts are inaccurate, substituting correct thoughts for erroneous ones and then gaining feedback to verify that his or her thoughts are accurate.

It would be a fascinating experience to have a computer printout of our own inner conversation for a day, let alone our counselee's. Most of us would be shocked by our inner conversations. We would be even more shocked to note some of the differences between what we say to ourselves inwardly and what we say to others in outward conversation. Most of us talk to others quite differently than we talk to ourselves.

We tend to respond more objectively to others but talk to ourselves in an unrealistic self-depreciating way.

Automatic Thoughts

Many thoughts are automatic. They jump into our consciousness without any planning or conscious prompting. Consider the characteristics of automatic thoughts.

First of all, an automatic thought is a specific message. A young woman who is afraid of being rejected by men tells herself, "He isn't interested in me. I'm not attractive enough."

Often an automatic thought surfaces not in a complete form but in a shorthand manner. It may take the form of a visual image or just a few words. The automatic thought may be a brief memory of something that occurred in the past, or it could be a series of disconnected words. A word or a series of short telegraphic phrases may serve as a label or summary for an entire group of painful memories, fears, or self-degrading statements.

Automatic thoughts are usually believed regardless of how irrational or off the wall they appear. They may appear rational to the individual because they are very rarely checked out or verified. They fail to get tested and the more they occur, the more they are believed.

These thoughts are experienced spontaneously. They just pop into the mind and since they're there . . . why shouldn't they be true?

Another characteristic of automatic thoughts is the terminology of "must," "should," or "ought." These are what we call the "torture words" since they elevate guilt and lower self-esteem. "I should do this . . ." or "I must be a perfect mother . . ." or "I ought to be consistent and never make a mistake." When these words appear on the screen of a person's mind, they generate hopelessness.

Automatic thoughts have the unique characteristic of "awfulizing." These thoughts expect the worse, see the danger behind every bush and create intense anxiety. They can color our attitude for days.

Automatic thoughts are also difficult to stop. They may appear somewhat reasonable and since they just pop in, they may become camouflaged amidst our other thoughts. It's hard to put a leash on them since they tend to come and go at will.

Automatic thoughts are learned. A person listens to others and what they say about them and he believes those statements.

Distorted Thoughts

Distorted thinking comes in many packages. Our proficiency increases as we are able to assist others in identifying their distortions. The identification process is the first step in countering and eventually eliminating this type of thinking. Our goal is to break free from being a captive of our thoughts by bringing every thought captive under Christ. Let's consider the various distortions.

1. *Filtering* is one way our thoughts become distorted. Another way of stating this is tunnel vision. A person looks at one element of a situation while ignoring everything else. You might receive praise for a project you just completed. But at the same time a constructive, positive suggestion is given for the next project. Which do you dwell upon? Some would concentrate on the suggestion, reinterpret it and see it as a negative statement. A person may then tend to both magnify and "awfulize" the statement. Fears, losses, and irritations are then exaggerated. We all have our own tunnels. Some of us, for instance, are sensitive to anything that hints of loss, danger, or frustration. And when any of these occur, our filtering tape is activated.

2. *Polarized thinking* is another distortion. This is the tendency to see everything in extremes. There is no room for a middle ground. People are either bad or good. Thus if a person makes one mistake, he judges himself as imperfect, a loser, no good. One mistake and "it's all over."

3. A frequent distortion is *overgeneralization*. A conclusion is based on one incident or piece of evidence. A young man asks a girl out and is turned down. He thinks, "I'll never be able to get a date." If you ate clams one time and became ill, you would say, "I'll never be able to eat clams again." If a spouse broke a promise, the other person thinks, "I'll never

be able to trust him again." One bad experience means that in a similar situation, you can expect a repeat.

Absolute statements characterize overgeneralizations, "No one appreciates a thing I do,"; "I'll never be able to get this right"; "I guess I'll always be depressed!" "Nobody likes me anymore." Evidence to the contrary is ignored.

4. *Mind reading*—making snap judgments about situations or people—creates distortions. There is no evidence for what we believe except our belief that there is. Assumptions are made based on hunches, intuition, one or two past experiences, or some vague feelings.

"The Smith family didn't greet me after church because they didn't like the message." "I just know they don't want to come, so why invite them." The conclusions are made and set in concrete rather than being checked out.

5. *Catastrophizing* is making a mountain out of the mole-hill. A frequent beginning to this type of thinking is, "What if. . . ." This is the cry of the worrier. One small problem means a disaster is on the way. A car is stolen a half mile away. "What if ours is stolen . . . ?" And the person continues to talk and amplify the situation, making it larger and larger.

6. *Personalization* is the distortion of relating everything to you. If a family member is sad, you blame yourself. If another person feels hurt, you take the responsibility whether you were involved or not. A spouse makes the angry statement, "I wish people were more considerate . . ." and immediately you believe she is talking about you.

Comparison with others is a main feature of this distortion. "He is a better speaker than I am." "I'm the most ineffective minister in town." "I'm not the same caliber as the rest of those people." Your value is based upon a comparison with others. Each comparison has an effect upon your perception of your own value and worth.

7. *Emotional reasoning* is a very common distortion. If you feel something, it must be true. If you feel like a failure, you must be a failure. If you feel guilty, you must have violated your standard. All negative things which you feel about life, others, and yourself must be true. Why? Because you feel them. These feelings come from distorted thoughts and they

67

in turn reinforce the thoughts. The distorted pattern of thinking and feelings can be the biggest decepter a person has to contend with.

8. *Blaming* brings us relief and also distorted thinking. It's nice to know that someone is responsible. Especially someone else. In blaming, we see others as responsible and ease our own responsibility. If your feelings are hurt, someone else is responsible. If you're afraid, someone else is responsible for those feelings.

But others walk through life as blame collectors. They have an incessant need to be wrong.

9. *Shoulds* are very common distortions. This person operates with a set of very inflexible rules that are correct, indisputable, and absolute—any deviation is bad. Other people should "know this" or "do this." They should be a certain way, think a certain way. Shoulds are a form of self-inflicted suffering and pain, a form of emotional masochism.

10. *Always being right* leads to a constant pattern of defensiveness and distorted thinking. It requires that you expend consistent effort to prove that your perspective is *always* right. Others' opinions don't count and are not even heard. You never make mistakes, thus you are impossible to live with.[1]

Irrational Beliefs

All of us operate with different sets of shoulds or beliefs. Most emotional disturbances are created by irrational beliefs. Many of them are contrary to the Christian perspective and yet many Christians continue to hang onto them. Most of these believers can be divided into two categories.

First of all, many people believe that certain things *must* be present in a person's life or *must* happen for them to be happy or accept themselves. In fact, the belief is that these are absolutely necessary! They include success, approval, love, comfort, convenience, health, certainty, and justice.

Secondly, other elements are believed to be terrible, awful, and unbearable. These must *not* happen. If these things happen the person feels worthless and happiness is impossible.

These include failure, rejection, deprivation, discomfort, inconvenience, illness, uncertainty, and injustice.

One or more of these beliefs is the root cause for most emotional upsets in a person's life. On the following pages is a list of emotional upsets and the beliefs that could be the root cause. Look for these as you counsel adolescents and adults alike. They will be related to specific situations for each person.

How do you help people deal with their distorted thoughts and inner conversations? There are three basic approaches: the intellectual, the experiential, and the behavioral.

The intellectual approach involves identifying misconceptions, testing their validity, and then substituting more appropriate beliefs. The experiential exposes the counselee to experiences that have such an impact the person is able to change his or her misconceptions. This could involve interaction with other significant individuals. The behavioral approach tends to encourage development of specific types of behaviors that help the counselees see themselves in a new way. Teaching assertion techniques to individuals will help them see others and themselves in a more realistic manner because learning to be assertive builds self-confidence.

It is important to remember that each person you see will vary in his or her ability to respond to this inner conversation approach. It works best with those who have the capacity for introspection and reflection about their own thought life and beliefs. For others, you may need to respond more initially to their feelings or behavior and gradually teach them to become more aware of their thinking process. This is just another example of entering the individual's frame of reference or of speaking their language so you can communicate accurately with them.

As you work with Christians and non-Christians, they all want to make sense of their lives and their emotional responses. Your presentation of the approach that you will be taking with them will be accepted if your timing is accurate. It cannot be given too soon nor after several sessions. Letting the counselee know that you have a plan in mind based upon

EMOTIONAL UPSET	FALSE BELIEF
1. Anxiety that is related to oneself.	1. I *must* be right, successful, outstanding and pleasing. 2. I *must* not make mistakes, or fail, or displease others.
2. Anxiety that is related to others.	1. I *must* be accepted and loved by others. 2. People *must* do things my way and give me what I want. 3. I *must* not be rejected or deprived in any way.
3. Anxiety that is related to situations and events.	1. Situations and events *must* work out the way I want. 2. I *must* have a guarantee. 3. Frustrations and misfortunes and crises *must* not happen.
4. Personal depression.	1. I'm *hopeless*. 2. It's *hopeless* and *unbearable*. 3. I'll *never* be able to solve this difficulty or be happy.
5. Guilt, shame, or worthlessness.	1. I am *no good* for failing. 2. I am *terrible* because of what I didn't do. 3. I am *terrible* because of what I did do.
6. Self-punishment.	1. I *have* to pay for what I have done. 2. I *have* to pay for my sins. 3. God *could not* forgive this.
7. Withdrawal, nonassertiveness, or phobias.	1. I *must* not go. 2. I *must* avoid situations in which I might be seen as inadequate or may fail or not be seen as loving, pleasing, etc.

EMOTIONAL UPSET	FALSE BELIEF
8. Overrebelliousness, withdrawal, and lack of cooperation.	1. I *must* have my way. 2. I *must* not be around those who bother or frustrate me or deprive me.
9. Low frustration tolerance and/or irresponsibility.	1. It is *too difficult* for me to persevere. 2. It is *too hard* to do things the ways others want them. 3. Life *should* be easier. 4. God *should not* have allowed that to happen. 5. God is *unfair* and he *owes* me more.
10. Anger directed back at oneself.	1. I *should* have done more or better. 2. I *should* be doing things better. 3. I *should* be a better Christian by now. 4. I *shouldn't* have failed.
11. Anger at others.	1. They *shouldn't* have done that. 2. They *should* be doing what I want. 3. They *shouldn't* be doing what I asked them not to.
12. Hostility or even violence against others.	1. People are not good because they don't give me what I want. 2. Others are no good for what they did or said to me. 3. Others have to pay for what they did or didn't do.[2]

his or her needs and concerns will reassure the person that something good is going to occur. Even if you take just two minutes to explain this approach, it can be reassuring and will not contradict the basic principles of listening and tending to their concerns.

Tom had been in for several sessions of counseling when the following conversation occurred.

Counselor: Tom, you've been here for five sessions now and I am wondering how you are feeling about the changes you shared with me earlier.

Tom: I guess I feel that I'm starting to get a handle on these thoughts of mine. I never realized how much I talked to myself, but it's really apparent that I do. And I don't always like what I'm thinking.

Counselor: Are you experiencing some change in your thinking?

Tom: Oh yes, it's coming along. Each day I am countering more and more.

Counselor: Tom, this might be a strange and unexpected question, but I was wondering if you had thought about a graduation date? When would you like to be finished with your counseling? Why don't we consider setting a date?

Tom: Huh . . . that is different. I never thought of graduating from counseling before. How would I know when I'm ready though?

Counselor: Perhaps one way to determine that is when you are able to handle your life and your difficulties by yourself and rely upon the Lord without assistance from me. How does that feel to you?

Tom: I guess I could handle that. The thought is a bit scary, but I feel comfortable with it. In fact, the thought that I will be able to function better on my own is kind of exciting. Yeah, it is all right.

Counselor: Do you have any thought in mind about a date or would you like to think about it for a week?

Tom: Let me think about it this week and come up with a date. Would we just stop or sort of taper off?

Counselor: Oh, we would taper off, and you would always have the opportunity of coming back. And while you are thinking of a date, why not think about what needs to be accomplished in your life before you graduate. That will give us something to work toward.

Tom: Yeah, I could do that. I'll work on that this week and have it written out for you next time.

Brevity is Important

Another principle of the inner conversation approach to counseling is that it is quite brief. This is especially important in the local church where you have so many demands upon your time. Most cognitive-therapy- or inner-conversation-counseling approaches take from five to twenty-five sessions. You may be thinking, *I thought you said this was short term!* It is! Other more traditional forms can take months to years.

Occasionally a counselee may need to be seen longer, but for most situations this approach to counseling can be effective for both the client and your time demands. I know of some therapists who set a graduation date for counseling right from the initial session. It might be three months, six months, or a year but they meet that date! When people know that a completion date is on the horizon they seem to work harder and follow through with assignments.

Brief counseling such as this discourages the person from becoming too dependent on the counselor or minister. As much as possible, we need to encourage and build the counselee's self-sufficiency. When people know that the counseling will be relatively short term, they begin to realize that their problem can be overcome more quickly than they realized. When you specify a certain number of sessions and then an evaluation time, the person goes to work on the problem sooner.

Please do not think that this approach to counseling overrides the counselee's need to be listened to or receive empathy. You can only move as rapidly as the strength and ability of the counselee. Some of them arrive in a state of crisis and your approach with them is different from what I am suggesting here.[3] Other individuals come out of their crisis very quickly or are able to move ahead with this approach from the onset of counseling. Your sensitivity will help you determine your timing. But our sensitivity is often imperfect and marred because of the Fall. This points up the need for our reliance upon the prompting and direction of the Holy Spirit to guide our minds, our thoughts, our ears and our eyes to make the proper assessment and statements.

An approach to counseling that moves at a fairly brisk pace is task-oriented and focuses on problem-solving. Each statement needs to have a purpose and a rationale. Some guidelines for this approach have been formulated by two of the pioneers and refiners of this style, Aaron Beck and Gary Emery. Here are their strategies:

1. *Keep your approach simple.* Do not complicate the counselee's situation since complicating things prolongs their progress.

2. *Make your suggestions specific and concrete.* Avoid abstract explanations and keep your terminology simple, matching your perceptual bias.

3. *Stress the value of homework.* This improves the rate of change.

4. *Stay on the subject or concern.* Do not bring in your own concerns or irrelevant material. This is not the time to seek their feedback on your previous Sunday message.

5. *Use time-management procedures.* How can you make the counseling time more effective than it is? Review your notes from the time before and consider what can be accomplished during this next session. Have books, tapes, or written assignments available.

6. *Develop the mindset that this approach can accomplish much in a brief time.*

7. During the session, *focus on manageable items.* This builds hope. Even though the issue presented may not be resolved, the counselee gains insights and tools to handle it on his own. Encourage the counselee to prepare for the session by arriving early and by sitting in a quiet room to think about the session and pray asking God to enlighten his thinking and give him guidance for the session.[4]

TRUST AND ACCEPTANCE ARE NECESSARY

In order for the inner conversation approach to be effective there must be a positive relationship based on trust and acceptance between you and the counselee. The counselee must be able to talk openly about his or her inner concerns, turmoil, and hurts.

Many of those who have experienced counseling say that what helped them is the concern and warmth of the counselor or minister and the freedom to expose their hurts and problems. We have talked before about the importance of empathy and viewing the world from the counselee's perspective. Inner conversation counseling lends itself to this because of the emphasis on viewing the world from the person's perspective. Experiencing rapid relief from difficulties also helps enhance the empathy.

Ask the counselee for feedback about the session or how life is progressing through the suggestions. This builds the relationship as it enables you to discover what is helping and what isn't. If the individual reports back to you that he is getting worse instead of better, or the suggestions haven't worked, you don't need to become defensive. Listen to what the person is saying. The counselee may be right or it may just be evidence of some unrealistic expectations.

It Is a Team Approach

Inner conversation counseling uses the team approach. It is an alliance in which the counselee supplies you with raw data and you provide the structure and the guidance in how he or she can learn to solve problems. Your emphasis is on how to resolve the problems, and not personality change per se. There will be times when you provide the lead and times when the counselee provides the lead in discovering solutions. As the counselee grows, he or she will take more of the active role. How does this reciprocal relationship develop?

1. By allowing the counselee to reciprocate. Neither person is superior. You work together.

2. By avoiding hidden agendas. The procedures and techniques are open and explained. I can remember therapist Dr. William Glasser (author of *Reality Therapy*) sharing with us in training that he usually gives his clients his book to read so they know what he believes and what to expect. Even

some paradoxical techniques should be clearly spelled out with the counselee.

3. By designing homework together. Offer a suggestion and then ask the counselee if he or she thinks this might work and if he or she has any suggestions for altering the assignment.

4. By admitting your mistakes. If you say something inappropriate or miss catching what was shared, admit it. By doing this, you are relating openly to the person and also serving as a positive model.

QUESTIONS HELP CLARIFY THINKING

Inner conversation counseling uses the Socratic method. In this approach you will use questions as much as possible. This is the pure form of this counseling theory. When time is limited, you can use more statements and you can make reassuring statements and reflective and empathic responses. But the questions are very important. They are used to help the person become more aware of his or her thoughts, to examine those thoughts for distortions, to substitute more balanced thoughts, and to make plans to develop new thought patterns.

Drs. Beck and Emery suggest that good questions can establish structure, develop collaboration, clarify the counselee's statements, awaken the counselee's interest, build the therapeutic relationships, provide the counselor with essential information, open up the counselee's previously closed system of logic, develop the motivation to try out new behavior, help the counselee think in a new way about the problem, and improve the counselee's self-observation.[5]

STRUCTURE PROMOTES LEARNING

This approach (as you have probably guessed by now) is structured and directive. This in no way means being inflexible and nonempathic, however. By the counselor's providing some structure, the person is given a degree of certainty and reassurance, and learning is promoted. How is this done? Often an agenda for the session is worked out between minister and counselee. The counselee is asked what he or she would like to deal with in the session. As a minister, you have the freedom to bring up items you feel are pertinent as well. The two of you will need to decide what takes precedence. This also means that you, the counselor, need to think and pray about the counselee before the session begins.

It is also important to focus upon specific targets within the session. In a sense, you need to develop a treatment approach for each person who walks into your office, whether the counseling is premarital, marital, individual, or family. The stages in this counseling are very sequential. First, you will try to provide some relief for the person's distress. Secondly, teach the person how to recognize his or her distortions. Thirdly, teach the individual how to respond to distorted thoughts with logic and reason, and to check out new responses. Fourthly, help the counselee identify and modify long-held irrational beliefs and assumptions that underly his or her concerns.

In order to provide assistance, it is important to make sure that you understand what the person is sharing with you. You can do that by responding, after the individual has shared for a time, "What I hear you saying is . . . ," "What you seem to be saying is . . . ," or, "Does the difficulty seem to be . . . ?" You might ask, "Am I catching what you are saying?" or, "Am I hearing you correctly?" or, "Am I seeing this from your perspective?" depending upon whether the individual is kinesthetic, auditory, or visual. (You may need to return to chapter one and review this.)

Encourage the person to share his or her feelings and concerns about the counseling and what occurs during the time with you. This does not mean that you are constantly seeking affirmation for your ability and your ego but for the counselee's benefit. Let him or her know it is alright to correct you, to make suggestions, and to let you know that it isn't working. By doing this you are also modeling. "Don't refuse to accept criticism . . ." (Prov. 23:12 TLB). "It is a badge of honor to accept valid criticism" (Prov. 25:12 TLB). "A man who refuses to admit his mistakes can never be successful. But if he confesses and forsakes them, he gets another chance" (Prov. 28:13 TLB).

THE INNER CONVERSATION APPROACH IS PROBLEM-ORIENTED

The initial focus is on resolving the person's immediate difficulties. Later sessions will deal with responding differently to problems—baggage from the past—and making new plans for the future. Your role is to encourage the individual to identify and work on present problems. Some difficulties can only be identified and resolved during some of your sessions.

It is helpful to break problems down into smaller solvable increments or to deal with those issues in which some immediate assistance can occur. This is especially important in the early sessions of counseling. If you leave individuals hanging, at the end of the session they may feel greater distress.

There are four steps involved in the problem-solving approach. The *first* is to clearly identify and clarify the individual's problem. This is called conceptualization which is simply placing the person's situation in the proper context. Remember that you need to draw out from your counselees what problems mean to them. You may have your own perception or opinion, but the issue must be seen from the counselee's eyes.

The *second* step is to select a strategy or a specific plan. Without this, counseling can become erratic.

The *third* step is a central part or the strategy—the selection of tactics or techniques. Your strategy is a general approach in which the tactic is very concrete and specific. Numerous tactics and techniques are available to ministers and professional counselors alike. But the ability to select and personalize for the person you are ministering to is an art that comes only through time, personal knowledge and growth, and experience in counseling others. If you are just beginning your counseling ministry, you will tend to emphasize tactics and techniques, since that gives you a greater sense of security. As you gain experience you will move more toward conceptualization and general strategies. Remember the goal of your counseling: to help the person function without you and with dependence upon God through his Word.

The *fourth* step is to assess the effectiveness of the tactic. There are numerous strategies you can use, but you will need to adapt them to each person. Again Beck and Emery suggest several simple strategies.

1. *Use the strategy of simplifying throughout your counseling.* People tend to overcomplicate their difficulties. Keep it simple and specific. If your counselee is vague, uses generalizations and assumes things, your task is to help him or her learn to be on target.

2. *Design a strategy to work on a problem in the session.* This can involve tackling what the person is thinking right during the session itself.

3. *Encourage the counselee to try things that seem difficult.* For instance, the counselee may say, "I'm afraid to go to the party because I might see a person I'm trying to avoid." This person's fear is that he or she wouldn't be able to handle seeing a certain individual. Encourage him or her to go to the party by saying, "Well, what could you learn if you go as compared to what you would learn if you stayed home?" Your encouragement can cause the person to reconsider his or her approach.

4. *If what you are doing isn't working, do the opposite.* If you are stuck and cannot help a person change his way of thinking, join him. I recall a counselee who was sure that he was going to fail as a real estate broker and nothing I could do helped him give up that belief. So I said, "All right, let's say you are going to fail as a real estate broker. In fact, you're going to do a terrible job. Then what?" I went along with his assumption and attempted to help him prepare for being a failure. It was interesting to see him begin to change his mind. He became uncomfortable with the idea of being a failure.

5. *Be consistently persistent and patient.* Many individuals do not believe they can change nor do they have the tenacity necessary to follow through. They need your belief and steadfastness in order to gain this for themselves. They don't need our frustration and a defeatest attitude; they already have enough of that of their own.

6. *Divide and conquer.* Show your counselees that their difficulty is made up of three parts: thinking, feeling, and action. Then help them work on that part which can be changed. Often they are overwhelmed by all three.

7. *Encourage counselees to do the unexpected, to surprise themselves.* The person may have numerous objections, but your gently persistent questioning can alleviate this concern. Your standard questions will be, "What's the worst that can happen if you try this and fail? Will it be any worse than what is happening now?" [6]

TEACH A NEW WAY TO LIVE

This approach to counseling is based upon an educational model. A premise of this approach is that a person develops many of his problems because he has learned inappropriate ways of handling his life experiences. This also means that with practice a person can learn a new way of living. This is very consistent with the teaching of Scripture. You can use many teaching techniques in the process of counseling, such as giving information, assigning reading, doing written exercises, or listening to tapes.

Some of those with whom you work will need to be taught how to learn. I often ask people if they read much during the week. In some cases I feel the need to determine whether reading is uncomfortable for the counselee, if he or she is unable to read well. I have found that most of them can read but have not been in the habit. I let them know that our counseling sessions can be an opportunity for them to develop the practice of reading since a whole new world of insight and help is available to them through the printed page. I also let them know that I believe they are very capable of incorporating this new task into their lives. Remember, they need our belief in them since often they are lacking in positive belief in themselves.

THE INDUCTIVE METHOD AND HOMEWORK ARE IMPERATIVE

Homework will be a major part of your counseling. You will be teaching the person how to use the homework to reinforce and amplify the actual counseling sessions. You need to explain to each person the necessity and benefits of homework as well as discover the ways the individual may keep from succeeding with the assignments.

These then are the basic principles of the inner conversation approach to counseling.

CHAPTER FIVE

HELPING PEOPLE CHANGE THEIR THOUGHT LIVES

THEORY IS A NECESSARY PART of counseling. We need to know why we are doing what we are doing. But most of us are more concerned about the practical side: "How do I do it?" Hopefully this chapter will provide some answers to this honest and necessary question. The procedures suggested here are applicable to many of the most common issues brought to your office including depression, worry, feelings of rejection and inadequacy, anger, passivity, and suspicion. Consider the steps involved in bringing about lasting change in a person's thought life.

First of all, I would like to draw on biblical references that are basic to the entire process of counseling. Years ago I took a course from Dr. William Glasser at the Institute of Family Therapy. It was a very informative and helpful course and quite behavior oriented rather than dealing with the thinking process. I will never forget one of Dr. Glasser's main points. He said that before a person will make a change, he needs to make a value judgment about what he is doing. In other words, he needs to state whether he likes what he is doing or dislikes it, whether it is beneficial to him or detrimental. In simple terms, does the person *want* to change?

As I thought about this I was reminded of a passage in the fifth chapter of the Gospel of John. Jesus confronted the man at the pool who had been crippled for thirty-eight years and asked him a very strange question: "Do you want to be healed?" In other words, "Do you want to change?" By asking this question Jesus was forcing the man to make a decision about what was going to occur in his life. He asked the man to take responsibility for remaining sick or for being made well.

In any type of counseling the person must see that there is a choice to be made: to remain the same or to change, to grow. The counselee must make that choice before much progress will be seen.

In one way or another I am looking for an answer to this question with any person or couple I work with in counseling. Many counselees are not sure that they will be able to change and thus are not fully committed to putting forth the time and effort and pain that change necessitates. Change involves risk, and most of us are looking for a written guarantee. But risking means we have an opportunity to live a life of faith! The changes that take place may be different than we anticipated both in the time involved and the ends that result.

When a person is a believer in Christ, he has a head start on change. I believe that change is possible for a believer in Christ because our faith is an inward transformation, not just an outward conformity. Yet for many people outward conformity seems to be all they can achieve. The plan God has for our lives creates an inward change, which then moves outward. When Paul says, "My little children, of whom I travail in birth again *until Christ be formed in you* . . . (Gal. 4:19

KJV, italics added), he is telling us that we have to let Jesus Christ live life *in* and *through* us.

In Ephesians 4:23, 24 we are told "and be renewed in the spirit of your minds, and put on the new nature, created after the likeness of God in true righteousness and holiness." The new man has to be put on from the inside. We are able to put on the new man because God has placed Jesus Christ within us. We are to let him work within us. This means being open to the ministry of the Holy Spirit to remold us. This is the message our counselees need to hear and to grasp! Suggest to them after your first or second session that they read the third chapter of *Making Peace With Your Past* to help them come to grips with this question of change.[1]

DEVELOPING AWARENESS OF INDIVIDUAL THOUGHTS

As you begin your counseling, your initial goal will be to help the person restructure thinking by becoming more aware of his or her thought processes. You will need to teach the counselee that learning to catch or be sensitive to one's thoughts is basic to personal growth. Watch out for the assumption that this is all that may be needed. It is only the first step that will allow the counselee to become more objective.

Now and then you will find the counselee responding by saying, "I have a difficult time remembering what I was thinking. I just seem to plod along with my life and maybe I'm oblivious to what's going on inside of me. I can't remember what I was thinking during the week."

Begin to probe for what he or she is thinking while in your office. Begin making a list of these thoughts or, better yet, provide the individual with writing material so he or she can make a list. The visual impact of seeing their thoughts on paper makes it much more significant. Sometimes they will say, "This made a real difference. It gave me a different perspective." One man said to me, "Now I know why I behave like I do. I set myself up with these thoughts. Now I can see how off the wall I've been with my thinking."

I find it important to discover what the person's thought would mean if it were true or carried out to completion. For example:

Counselee: Well, I have discovered this week that, ah, I think a lot about, ah . . . well, being rejected. I'm really afraid that others will reject me. In fact I find myself saying to myself, *Oh! Oh! They won't like me. They won't want me around. I'm going to be rejected.*

Minister: Being rejected would mean. . . .

Counselee: Huh. That's a new thought. I guess being rejected would mean, oh, that something is wrong with me. I'm defective. It would hurt.

Translating whatever the person says into "this would mean . . ." helps the person see where his thoughts are leading.

Part of the purpose of this approach is to help the counselee take a more active role in life rather than reacting to it. You may be surprised at how many individuals can become aware of their thoughts just by being told to do so. An important step is teaching the individual to replace "why" questions with "how" questions. Many people ask, "Why am I depressed?" "Why am I so worried?" "Why am I feeling so upset?" "Why am I so angry?" "Why am I so anxious?" "Why do I feel so far away from God?" These questions do not bring about a resolution of the difficulty. "Why" questions often go unanswered or we argue with the answer!

What happens when these questions are changed from why to how? "How am I making myself depressed?" "How am I making myself so worried?" "How am I making myself so upset?" "How am I making myself so angry?" "How am I creating my anxiety?" "How am I making myself feel so far away from God?" Awareness comes when questions are asked in this fashion.

After a person has learned to identify his or her faulty thinking, the next step is learning to correct the distortions and restructure the thinking. Here is where you may need to do some experimenting. You will need to discover the most effective approach for each person because each person is unique. You can use a variety of approaches to change thought life. Even though you are primarily concerned with changing thoughts, you can use behavioral approaches, affective (feeling) or cognitive approaches that deal directly with the thoughts. Whatever approach you use you should incorporate the use of imagery and prayer in order for positive change to occur. Let's look now at some strategies and techniques.

A very simple approach and one that works well with those unable to recapture some of their specific thoughts is to have them count their thoughts as they occur. This assists in several ways. It helps counselees feel as though they are gaining some control over their situations, it helps them recognize how automatic their thoughts are, and it helps give them a better perspective on their thinking. This is a beginning step in recognizing how their thoughts affect emotions and behavior.

Suggest that the counselee keep a 3 × 5 card and make a mark every time a thought occurs. This doesn't have to be done every waking moment but there can be a sampling during the day or a count when one is especially distressed.

As the person begins to record his thoughts, you will want to help him identify his false beliefs. Don't label them as such to begin with; simply help him decipher what he is thinking. Later you will be able to help him label his own beliefs as well as consider the consequences of those beliefs. One method of identification is to focus on and verbalize the thoughts that occur before, during, and after the difficulties the person has described. For example, a wife is upset about her marriage, her husband's lack of involvement with the family, and his long work hours. You will need to encourage her to discuss her self-talk concerning her husband's noninvolvement. Some questions you might ask are:

1. What thoughts go through your mind right before you start to feel upset? Do you tell yourself that your husband *should* be more involved in the family life and with you? Do you tell yourself that he doesn't love you? Do you tell yourself that he shouldn't be staying away as much as he does and that you cannot stand it? Do you tell yourself that he should treat you better?

2. What thoughts do you have about yourself in this situation? Do you say, "If I were a better wife, he would want to be around me"?

3. What thoughts go through your mind when your husband does not come home or when he doesn't respond to you? Do you feel he shouldn't be doing that? Do you say it is unfair?

4. What thoughts do you have about the future of your marriage? Do you think that it is never going to change? Do you wonder why your husband is mistreating you in this way?

By asking questions like these you can usually identify the specific beliefs that are causing or continuing the unhappiness.

If such questions do not give sufficient information, however, there are other information gathering approaches you can use. If the woman cannot identify specific beliefs associated with her problem, you could ask questions that suggest she may be holding onto a specific belief or experiencing a certain feeling and behaving in a particular way. Some questions are:

"Could it be that you are thinking that this is unfair?"

"Could it be possible that you are quite angry about this?"

"Is it possible that you are getting down on yourself over this?"

This will help the woman see the relationship between what she is thinking and what she is feeling or doing.

Another approach is to express how "another person" might think, feel, and behave if you were she. "Well, if I were in that situation, I might begin to think that . . . and then I would probably do . . ." By demonstrating how another individual might respond, you may be able to help her identify and express what she is thinking and feeling.

As she becomes aware of her thoughts and the relationship between her thoughts, feelings, and behavior, and the ensuing consequences, ask her to keep a journal of all of these elements. This will help her become aware of the frequency of her thoughts and the consequences of her faulty thinking.

THE VALUE OF ASKING QUESTIONS

A unique feature of this approach to counseling is the use of questions in your interaction with the counselee. For the past decade these questions have been suggested in numerous resources and each time they are presented with a bit more refinement.

Questions help counselees correct their faulty thinking and logic because they bring the counselee to the place where he will be able to use these same questions for himself and gain control over his thought life. Below is just a sampling of the kinds of questions you can use.

1. *What is the evidence for or against this thought?* You are asking for evidence for the truth or the falseness of this belief. It is one of the most frequently asked questions in counseling and an easy question for the counselee to learn to use.

2. *Where is the logic for this belief?* As a person looks at the belief in a different fashion, he or she begins to see that this belief is often not valid.

3. *Are you oversimplifying the situation?* One man I worked with believed that if he made one mistake in his sermon the positive points would be ignored or forgotten; the people would only remember the mistake. Through our discussion he began to realize that all of us make these mistakes and it wouldn't have that drastic an effect upon the congregation.

4. *Could you be confusing the facts with your perception of the facts?* As the person begins to look at his own interpretation, the situation may be clarified. An additional question might be: "If someone else were there, or if I were there, how would I see it?"

5. *In what way might you be thinking in all-or-nothing terms?* After the person responds, probe the thinking further by saying, "Let's assume that instead of everyone rejecting you in your family, only one person rejects you and the others accept you. Might that be a possibility?"

6. *As you hear yourself thinking, are you finding some words that are extreme or even exaggerated?* The absolutes come into this category such as *never, all, always, no one, everyone.*

7. *You know, most of us use some defense mechanisms from time to time. Could you be using some denial, or projection, or rationalization? Let's look at some other possible reasons for how you are behaving.*

8. *Are you basing what you are doing on facts or on feelings? Can you give me an example?* Many individuals use feelings to validate themselves. They must become conscious of that tendency.

9. *What is your source of information for that belief?* I

am amazed at the number of individuals who take at face value what they hear from unreliable sources such as the radio, TV, or friends. Most of us are influenced more than we realize by television and by information fed to us by the media. And we tend to believe what we hear. We do this in Christian circles also. An example of this is the statement I have heard for years that Christian couples who attend church have a significantly lower divorce rate. In fact, one statistic I have heard is that only five couples out of one hundred who attend church divorce. (Unfortunately this is not true.) I'm sure I have bothered some individuals by asking them for their source and usually they cannot substantiate what they have said.

There are many additional questions you can use to assist your counselee. You may even want to ask the individual, "What questions do you think you could ask yourself that would help you look at your beliefs and thoughts."

GUIDELINES FOR USING QUESTIONS

There are some guidelines to follow when you ask questions. First of all, *do not answer the question for the individual.* If the person is hesitant about responding to the question, allow him or her to say, "I don't understand," instead of your assuming the person is confused. Sometimes he needs a bit of time to sort through his thoughts in order to respond. Or you could rephrase the question. If the counselee gives a very general response to your question, say, "Could you be more specific?"

Attempt to *ask specific and concrete questions.* General questions have their place such as, "How did your week go?" or "How have you been feeling the past few days?" Making your questions more specific, however, will elicit more helpful responses. Personally I feel more comfortable balancing my questions with statements that accomplish the same goal.

Be sure you have a good reason for any question you ask. If you were to listen to a tape recording of one of your sessions, could you give the specific purpose for each question you asked? What were you after? Was the question asked for the growth and benefit of the counselee? Sometimes I will ask a question for impact or to have the individual or couple think about the question for a week.

The purpose of any question you ask should be *to build both the relationship between you and the counselee and to help the person learn to solve problems* (not just this problem). Your tone of voice is the greatest conveyor of concern and care in the counseling office. Listen to your inflections, your volume, the quality of your voice coupled with your nonverbal language which should show even more concern and caring.

Space your questions so the individual does not feel pressured or under attack. Each individual has his or her own timing when it comes to formulating responses. If you are a person who tends to think very rapidly, you may expect others to respond in a like manner. Adapt to the counselee's rate of thinking and speaking so a level of comfort is established.

Use questions to gain information and to uncover thinking below the conscious, surface level. Encourage the counselee to go further and further in his or her responses. A simple question such as, "Can you think of anything else?" or "Why don't you take some time and see if anything else comes to mind?" can be very useful. Sometimes asking the same question in a different manner enables him or her to respond in greater detail.

Where Is the Evidence?

There are four basic approaches in your use of this technique with your counselees.

The first one is to ask: *Where is the evidence?* As you interact with your counselees, help them discover if any evidence exists for the beliefs they hold. Sometimes it helps to suggest they write down the evidence. A minister I worked with often had the idea that the people thought him boring and wished he would leave the church. Naturally, he ended up feeling rejected, depressed, and often immobilized. As we looked at his list of evidence for his belief we found that not only was evidence lacking, there was a great deal of evidence to the contrary. Often these negative thoughts are a reflection of our own feelings about ourselves rather than the feelings of others.

Providing information for counselees can help them challenge their beliefs. Those who are fearful, or who wonder if what they are experiencing is normal, benefit from this approach. I talk with so many who are experiencing some type of crisis and I often use a crisis sequence chart which shows the four stages of a crisis and what occurs at each stage. I hand it to them and ask them to show me where they are at that time with reference to the chart. They are usually able to identify their place, but so many say, "You mean, what I'm going through is normal?"

"Yes," I reply, "and not only is it normal, and most people go through this same sequence, did you notice that you will be coming out of it in a few weeks?" Relief and hope now become a part of their life.[2]

Another way to help the counselee answer the question, *Where is the evidence?* is to test out the person's belief. If the belief is, "I'm so upset, I can't do anything around the house," test it out by giving the person two simple tasks to perform. If the belief is "I'm so upset I can't even read the Bible," hand the person your Bible and ask him or her to read a passage. You can set up other experiments to test the counselee's beliefs. Often though when you suggest the person test his or her belief, you will hear, "Oh, I guess I don't need to try it. It just seems to be that way."

What Is Another Viewpoint?

A second basic approach is to ask: *What's another way of looking at this situation?* What is an alternative approach or response? Again, writing can be beneficial, seeing the alternative explanation in writing brings home the reality of the situation. Some people may be willing to carry a notebook and write down their thoughts on one side of the page and list the correction of the belief on the other. This will benefit the counselees and will also let you see what occurs during the week.

Often I say something like this to a counselee: "You know, most of us have times in our lives when we allow ourselves to be overly influenced by our thoughts. Even irrational thoughts. You appear to be struggling with such thoughts.

There are a few things I would like you to remember. Let me share them with you verbally and don't be concerned if you don't remember everything. I have them written down for you so you can take them with you to review and use during this next week. This will be part of your homework. I would like to encourage you to remember that these spontaneous or automatic thoughts that pop into your mind are reflections of some of your inner feelings. Try to identify the feeling you have whenever the thought comes. This will help you remember the actual thought if you have a hard time remembering it.

"The next step is to get rid of these thoughts by answering them. Talk back to them by giving a different interpretation of each situation. In fact, you may want to come up with several different interpretations. Here is a list of twenty questions that will help you with this process. I would like you to look over the list for a few moments now and let me know how you feel about the questions. Does this sound all right to you?"

Then I hand them the listing of questions below and wait for their response. I encourage you to have copies made so you can use them with your counselees.

1. *What is the evidence?* Ask yourself the question: "Would this thought hold up in a court of law? Is it circumstantial evidence?" Just because your mailman misses delivering the mail one day does not mean that you cannot count on anything. Just because you tripped walking into your new class and everyone laughed does not mean that you will trip again or that they think you are a clod.

2. *Am I making a mistake in assuming what causes what?* It is often difficult to determine causes. Many people worry about their weight, and if they gain weight they make the assumption that "I don't have any will power." But is that the only reason? Could there be other causes such as glandular imbalance, using eating as a means to deal with unhappiness, etc.? We do not know the causes of obesity for certain. The medical profession is still studying the problem.

3. *Am I confusing a thought with a fact?* Do you say, "I've failed before so why should this be any different?" Calling yourself a failure and then believing it does not mean the

label you've given yourself is accurate. Check out the facts with yourself and with others.

4. *Am I close enough to the situation to really know what is happening?* You may have the thought, *The management of my company does not like my work and they are probably planning on getting rid of me in the next three months.* How do you know what management is thinking? Are you on the management level? Is your assumption correct? Is your source of information accurate? How can you determine the facts?

5. *Am I thinking in all-or-none terms?* Many people see life as black or white. The world is either great or lousy. People are either all good or all bad. All people are to be feared. Again, where did you get this idea? What are the facts?

6. *Am I using "ultimatum" words in my thinking?* "I must always be on time or no one will like me." That is an unfair statement to make about yourself or anyone else. Notice the following example of how our words can create problems. It is the inner conversation of a woman whose boyfriend left her for another woman. This woman was attending college where numerous other men were available.

Negative Thoughts	Answers
He shouldn't have left me for someone else.	I don't like it, but he should have left because he did. For all the reasons I don't know of, he should have left. I don't have to like it, just accept it.
I need him.	I want him back, but I don't need him. I need food, water, and shelter to survive. I don't need a man to survive. Thinking in "needs" makes me vulnerable.
This always happens to me, and it will never change.	Just because it happened in one case doesn't mean it has happened or will happen in every case.
This is terrible, awful, horrible.	These are labels I add to the facts. The labels don't change anything and they make me feel worse.
I must have someone to love me.	It's nice to love and be loved, but making it a condition to be happy is a way of putting myself down.

Negative Thoughts	Answers
I'm too ugly and too fat to find anyone else.	"Too" is a relative concept, not some absolute standard. Thinking like this is self-defeating and stops me from trying.
I can't stand being alone.	I can stand difficulties—as I have in the past. I just don't like them.
I made a fool out of myself.	There's no such thing as a fool. Foolishness is only an abstraction, not something that exists. This mislabeling doesn't do me any good and makes me feel bad.
He made me depressed.	No one can make me feel depressed. I make myself depressed by the way I'm thinking.[3]

7. *Am I taking examples out of context?* A woman overheard the conversation of an instructor talking to another instructor about her. She thought the instructor said she was rigid, pushy, and dominant. Fortunately, she checked out the conversation with one of the two instructors and discovered that she had been described as having high standards and determination. The words were spoken in a positive context, but because of her tendency to think the worst, distortion occurred.

8. *Am I being honest with myself?* Are you trying to fool yourself or make excuses or put the blame on others?

9. *What is the source of my information?* Are your sources accurate, reliable, trustworthy, and do you hear them correctly? Do you ask them to repeat what they say and verify it?

10. *What is the probability of my thought occurring?* Perhaps your situation is so rare an occurence there is little chance of your worry coming true. One man had the thought that because he had missed work for two days he would be fired. After he thought about it he said, "Well, I've worked there for several years and have a good record. When was the last time anyone was fired for missing two days' work? When was the last time they fired anyone?"

11. *Am I assuming every situation is the same?* Just because

you didn't get along at the last two jobs does not mean that you will not get along at your new one. Just because you failed algebra the first time around does not mean you will fail it the second time.

12. *Am I focusing on irrelevant factors?* Of course there are problems in the world and people are physically and mentally sick, and there is crime, etc. What can you do to eliminate these problems by sitting around worrying about them or becoming depressed over them? How else could you use your thinking time in a more productive manner?

13. *Am I overlooking my strengths?* People who worry or who are depressed definitely overlook their positive qualities. They do not treat themselves as a friend. They are hard on themselves and focus upon their supposed defects instead of identifying their strengths and praising God for them. It is important not only to list your strengths but also recall times in your past when you were successful.

14. *What do I want?* This is a question I ask people over and over again in counseling. What goals have you set for your life? What do you want out of life? How do you want your life to be different? What is the fear that you want to be free from at this point in your life?

15. *How would I approach this situation if I were not worrying about it?* Would I tend to make it worse than it is? Would I be as immobilized by the problem as I am now? Imagine how you would respond if you believed that you had the capabilities of handling it.

16. *What can I do to solve the situation?* Are my thoughts leading to a solution of this problem or making it worse? Have I written down a solution to the problem? When was the last time I tried a different approach?

17. *Am I asking myself questions that have no answers?* Questions like "How can I undo the past?" "Why did that have to happen?" "Why can't people be more sensitive?" or, "Why did this happen to me?" Often questions like these can be answered with the question "Why not?" What if something terrible happens? Why spend time asking yourself unanswerable questions?

18. *What are the distortions in my own thinking?* The first

step in overcoming errors is to identify them. Do you make assumptions or jump to conclusions? What are they? The best way to deal with an assumption is to check it out. Look for the facts.

19. *What are the advantages and disadvantages of thinking this way?* What are the advantages of worrying? List them on a piece of paper. What are the advantages of thinking that people don't like you? What is the benefit of *any* type of negative thinking?

20. *What difference will this make in a week, a year, or ten years?* Will you remember what happened in the future? Five years from now who will remember that your shirt was buttoned wrong? Who really cares? We believe that our mistakes are more important to other people than they really are. If people choose to remember ten years from now, something you said or did that bothered them, that's their problem, not yours.[4]

How Responsible Are You?

The third approach in the use of questions is, *"How much responsibility are you willing to take to solve the problem?"* For some time, I worked with a salesman who was having difficulty closing his sales. Those he did close often fell through later on. His automatic thoughts were, *I am a terrible salesman. There must be something wrong with me. I'm 34 years of age and I am never going to get anywhere.* He felt totally responsible for his situation and said that he did! Ask your counselees how responsible they feel. Have them rate it from zero to 100 percent.

The salesman and I looked together to see what was affecting the actual outcome of his sales and discovered that the company could not meet its production deadlines. They did not have a good service policy, and the competitor's product was more efficient while being priced similarly. As we considered these and other factors, he began to relax and develop a different perspective about himself. One month after this his competition called and offered him a job and a substantial raise because they liked what they saw whenever they ran into him. He accepted the position and was very successful.

He finally had a company that would back him up and support him.

As you minister to people in counseling, you can either teach them about their thought life or use the discovery method. Some individuals respond best to the discovery method. When you help the person to develop realistic ideas and beliefs through discovery, you do not openly state what appears to be the better way of thinking. Instead, you structure questions in such a way that the person gradually recognizes exceptions to his false beliefs. Here is a variation of a discovery approach suggested by Lembo, Johnson and Matross.[5]

1. Identify the person's false beliefs. An example might be: "When I make a mistake, it makes me feel worthless and depressed."

2. Ask the person about specific past and present behaviors and events that are related to this false belief. You could begin with a general approach like, "Let's talk about some of your reactions to things. I would like you to give me examples of some important things you have done in the past month and how each one worked out for you." Be sure to ask for specifics and have the individual stick to answering your questions.

3. Now ask detailed questions about the circumstance, thoughts, or behavior patterns for one problem example that your counselee claims supports his false belief. If he responds with, "I lost an important sale the other day which made me depressed," ask questions like, "What were your thoughts immediately after you discovered that your sale fell through?" "What did you think this meant?" Summarize aloud the person's response to each of your questions.

4. Now determine the kinds of behaviors or events that would actually contradict the person's false beliefs. In the example above, any mistake or failure which did not make him upset or depressed would actually contradict his false belief that mistakes create feelings of depression and worthlessness.

5. Ask the person for a very specific example of a potentially upsetting experience like, "Tell me about a time when you made a mistake but did not become depressed." Ask detailed questions about the circumstances, thoughts, behaviors, and consequences of this example. Again be sure you summarize

each of the person's responses to your questions out loud.

6. This next step is very important. Compare and contrast the person's thoughts, feelings, behavior, and consequences during a time when he became depressed and a time when he did not become depressed. Help him see the difference between the two.

For example, you might say: "On one hand, when you make an error, or tell yourself. . . , or view yourself as. . . , you tend to feel. . . . On the other hand, when you make a mistake, or tell yourself . . . , or view yourself as . . . you tend to feel. . . . Why do you feel you have the emotional response that you do? Do you see the connection between your thoughts and feelings?

7. Ask the person to reexamine his original belief in light of what he has now discovered about the connection between his thoughts and feelings. "In light of what we have now discussed, what do you believe about mistakes and failures making you depressed and worthless?" Ask the person to specify how the old belief can be modified. Ask about the potential consequences of this new belief.

After you have read the chapters on imagery and prayer, return to this Discovery Approach and decide at what point you will use either prayer or imagery. Since homework is an important ingredient in the counseling process, the following are two assignments you might give.

1. *Eliminating a false belief.* The purpose of this assignment is to refute a false belief that has been affecting the person's life. It is a relatively simple exercise but must be completed in writing. It will take a commitment of ten minutes per day. Ask the counselee to write a thorough answer to each of four questions.

- What major false belief do I want to eliminate?
  Example: It would be awful and upsetting if I did not get the new job I applied for last week.

- What reliable evidence can I discover that makes this idea false?

Example: It would be unfortunate if I did not get the job, but it would not be overwhelming. I would prefer getting the job, but there are other jobs available. I will be able to handle it and look for another job.

- If what I want does not occur (getting the job) or the undesirable does happen, what is the worst that might happen to me?

    Example: I wouldn't have a job when I wanted to and I wouldn't have the money I want. I might have to explain to others why I'm not working. I would have to go through the process of applying and filling out more work applications and that's a pain in the neck.

- If what I want doesn't occur or if the undesirable thing does occur, what are the satisfying things I can do as an alternative?

    Example: Well, I could spend the free time with friends or parents or do some leisurely reading when I'm not looking for a job. I can ask the place where I didn't get the job what I would need to do or improve upon in order to obtain a similar job. I can use this experience to rely more upon God and seek his will for the right job. I can even thank him for closing this door.

Some counselees find it helpful to write these questions on a 3 × 5 card and carry the card around with them. Whenever their thoughts stray back to their false belief, they bring out the card and reread all of the steps just described. This helps them reinforce their new pattern of thinking.[6]

2. *Thought Evaluation Worksheet.* The Thought Evaluation Worksheet can help your counselee uproot false beliefs and replace them with proper objective beliefs. There are many variations to this approach. I would encourage you to experiment and adapt it to the particular individuals to whom you minister in your own counseling situation. Here is one example of such a worksheet.

Situation
[*Briefly describe the undesirable situation which upsets you.*]

I can't live in an apartment with two other friends my first year of college because my parents won't allow it.

Correct Analysis of the Situation
[*This is done to determine whether the description you have given of your situation is accurate.*]

The situation is true. They won't let me move and if I were to do so, my support would be cut off.

Self-talk or inner conversations
[*List the specific statements that you tell yourself when you think about this unfair and undesirable situation.*]

Thought challenges and alternative interpretations
[*This is the time to challenge the truth and helpfulness of each item of self-talk and list alternative statements that would accurately describe the meaning of your situation and be in your own best interest to believe.*]

1. This is awful.

1. Where is the evidence that this is awful? It is disappointing but is not the end of the world. I have handled other disappointments before. I may discover later on that moving wouldn't have worked out.

2. This is unfair.

2. What is unfair about this? That depends on how I interpret it. Fairness is not the issue here.

3. My parents are just trying to control me and they don't trust me.

3. How do I know that my parents are trying to control me? That's mindreading. Have I asked them if that is their purpose? They have trusted me many times and have given me freedom. I can write down the reasons they gave me for not moving in with my friends.

101

4. My friends will find someone else to room with and then I won't ever get to be with them in an apartment.	4. How do I know my friends will find someone else? What if they do? Does that mean they are no longer my friends? Where is the evidence that I will never get to be with them? I am feeling sorry for myself and looking for the worst consequences.
5. I always miss out on good times like that.	5. I don't always miss out. I have lots of good times. I am allowing this one disappointment to erase all of my memories of good times. Here is a list of some of them.

Here is yet another illustration of a five-step process that can be used with your counselees.

The five steps are: Identifying the Situation, Negative Thoughts, Resulting Feelings, Resulting Behavior, and Counters. Here are two examples:

SITUATION: I am unhappy because someone very close to me is graduating and going off to college in another state.
NEGATIVE THOUGHT: I should be happy all the time. Christians should not be unhappy.
RESULTING FEELINGS: Unworthiness, shame.
RESULTING BEHAVIOR: I didn't express to my friend that I will miss her. My friend gets the impression that I don't care that she's leaving.
COUNTERS (arguments against the negative thought):

1. That's nonsense! I can't think of one biblical character who was happy all the time!
2. That negative thought is a great way to lose friends fast!
3. That's dumb! I'm trying to be God.
4. Whoever told me that Christians should never be unhappy? Certainly my pastor has never suggested it!

SITUATION: I'm sitting alone at home. Several things went wrong for me this week. I would like to be able to get some support from someone. I want to tell my family what has happened, but I'm not sure of their response. I don't want to be laughed at.

NEGATIVE THOUGHT: Strong people don't ask for help.
RESULTING FEELINGS: Extreme loneliness, dejection.
RESULTING BEHAVIOR: I stayed in my apartment all weekend. I even started to drink.
COUNTERS:

1. Moses asked for help from God continually. He asked God for help to be able to speak to the Israelites. And Moses became one of the greatest leaders Israel ever had.
2. Other people I know ask for help continually.
3. I often help other people with their problems. Am I not entitled to the same?
4. It's okay not to be perfect.
5. This thought only hurts me.
6. Drinking isn't the answer.

Assumptions are at the heart of negative self-talk. Identifying negative assumptions and their consequences can be an important corrective technique. Here is an illustration from a client who lived under the unrealistic belief that "I must always do what others expect me to do." Needless to say, his life was one of feeling pressured and manipulated. After completing the following form, this counselee was very aware of the cost of following this assumption. Here is his description. This format is one you can adapt and use with your counselees.

ASSUMPTIONS AND THEIR CONSEQUENCES

Assumptions—"I must always do what others expect me to do."

Advantages of believing this and acting upon it	Disadvantages of believing this and acting upon it.
1. If I can meet other people's expectations, I feel like I am in control. I like this. It feels good.	1. When I do this, I sometimes compromise. I do things that I really don't want to do. They're not the best for me.

ASSUMPTIONS AND THEIR CONSEQUENCES

2. I feel secure when I please others.

2. When I do this, I end up never knowing if others like me just for who I am. I end up being their slave, doing things for them in order to insure that I am accepted.

3. I don't have to figure things out for myself since I depend on others telling me what to do.

3. Wow. This sure lets others control me. I give them power over me. I'm not really in control.

4. I don't have to be concerned about people not liking me or accepting me.

4. But do they really like me for me? How do I know that? Always being the good guy limits me because if I do what I want to do, what will they think? I live in fear of their rejection!

5. I don't have much conflict in my life since I'm such a people pleaser.

5. Sometimes people do disapprove of me in spite of my trying to please them, and then I feel rotten. *I can't do anything right* is my thought.

6. People take advantage of me because they are thinking of themselves rather than me. I get the short end of the deal. I do get angry at them for what they do and have negative thoughts about them.

3. *Creating alternative interpretations.* Here are some additional suggestions to use as you work on creating alternative interpretations, taken from one of my earlier books.

Typical misbeliefs of those who suffer from low self-esteem:

- The way to be liked by other people is to be what others want me to be and to do what is most pleasing to them.
- It is more Christian to please other people than to please myself.

- Other people have the right to judge my actions.
- It is wrong and un-Christian to think my own needs are important when compared to the needs of others.
- It is wrong not to forget my own wants in order to please friends and family when they want me to.
- Pleasing others is an insurance policy that guarantees that people will be nice to me in return. When I am in great need they will forget their own needs and help me.
- When other people are displeased with me, it is impossible to get one moment's peace or happiness.
- Approval from everyone else is absolutely necessary to my feelings of well-being and peace of mind, since God doesn't want me to be happy unless everyone else is approving of me.
- Being what other people want me to be is the only way to be liked.
- Pleasing others and doing what they expect of me is the only way to win friends.

By contrast, here are some beliefs and thoughts that are positive, balanced, and healthy:

- It is *not* necessary to be liked by everyone.
- I do not have to earn anyone's approval or acceptance to be a person of worth.
- I am a child of God. I am deeply loved by him, and I have been forgiven by him; therefore I am acceptable. I accept myself.
- My needs and wants are as important as other people's.
- Rejection is *not* terrible. It may be a bit unpleasant, but it is not terrible.
- Not being approved or accepted is *not* terrible. It may not be desirable, but it is not terrible.
- If somebody doesn't like me, I can live with it. I don't have to work feverishly to get him or her to like me.
- I can conquer my bad feelings by distinguishing the truth from misbelief.

- It is a misbelief that I must please other people and be approved by them.
- Jesus died on the cross for me so that I can be free from the misbelief that other people decide my value.

What If It Happens?

The fourth basic approach is quite different but it is effective. It is called *So what if it happens?*

You might say to the person, "Let's assume that this might occur. First of all, what is the probability of it happening? Let's figure it out on a percentage basis. Secondly, assuming it happens, is it that terrible? Is it really a catastrophe? Thirdly, do you really have the ability to keep it from happening? Can you prevent it? Let's say now that it occurs. Are you incapable of handling it? Where is the evidence for that? What other crisis have you experienced in your life? Tell me how you handled it."

These and similar questions can take the individual from the desire to flee and bring him or her to the point of facing the experience; this, in turn, can lessen the fear.

There are many practical techniques and approaches you can use as you minister to others. But all of these suggested can be much more effective when imagery and prayer are integrated. Let's consider these as you read on.

CHAPTER SIX

THE USE OF IMAGERY IN COUNSELING

WHAT COMES TO YOUR MIND when the word *imagery* is mentioned? Is imagery some mysterious, cultic practice that leads to deeper psychological and spiritual problems? Or is it a gift from God to be used in a positive way? How knowledgeable are you of its potential? What is the source of your information concerning its use?

Fantasy and daydreams are characteristics of human life; our ability to imagine sets us apart from animals. You daydream and so do I. This is imaging. Daydreams have positive potential as well as negative. They have been responsible for some of our greatest discoveries. Thomas Edison did not just sit down and invent the light bulb. He first laid on the couch in his workshop and filled his mind with fantasies. Debussy created some of his music by viewing reflections of the sun on the river. Imaging is a gift from God and is the mother of ambition and creativity. When you see a great cathedral, remember that at one time it existed as an idea in someone's mind. That imagery was translated into reality.

Fantasy can rescue us from drudgery or lead us to create a masterpiece; one is tied to escape, the other to accomplishment. Fantasy can also be used to help heal our negative memories and free us from self-condemnation. It can be used as a powerful magnet to draw out our strengths and abilities to unlock problems and to tear down barriers blocking progress and growth.

What images are in your mind today? What is their purpose and how are you using them?

Imagination is a creative function each of us possesses. People do vary in how much they use their imagination and the way in which it is used, but we all use it. What would it be like for a pastor to be able to see all of the fantasies and imagery that occur during one of his sermons on Sunday morning?

Sometimes we use our imagery in a negative way. Have you ever started the day irritated over something your spouse did or said to you? During the day you dwelt on it, visualizing what you were going to do and say when you next saw your spouse. You went through a mental rehearsal, time and time again. When your spouse made an appearance you were ready with a well-rehearsed description of the offense and your displeasure! In fact, your spouse may have been amazed at the refinement of your presentation, but it was nothing to be amazed at, for you had prepared well. What if you were to take that same effort and energy and put it to use in a highly constructive, positive manner?

The people you see in counseling have been using their imagination in negative or faulty ways, which is one reason they are having difficulty and why their problems are so entrenched.

I have read numerous books and articles on this subject. I have also taken seminars on the use of imagery in therapy and pain control, and have learned there is much discussion and some controversy over its usage. Why? Because with any approach, whether it be biblical or secular, imagery can be misused, over-used, or totally rejected and not even given a hearing. Consider with me a definition of imagery, a scriptural perspective, and how imagery can be used constructively.

Imagery is actually the basis for our thought processes. It is a way to process information. The words we first develop as an infant probably occur because we first had images in our mind.

People who can describe images with a great deal of accuracy often become authors or story tellers. If you have ever listened to "The Prairie Home Companion" on the radio, you know that the director and host, Garrison Keillor, has a unique ability as a story teller. In each program Keillor tells a story about a fictitious small town named "Lake Wobegon," and he tells it so well that when you listen you feel as though you were in that small community experiencing what is being described. He paints mental pictures for us.

The greatness of Shakespeare and other authors lies in part in the tremendous range of their vocabulary—words that evoke our sense of smell, touch, taste, hearing, or sight. These create images in our minds.

WHAT IS IMAGING?

Imaging is the forming of mental pictures or images. We have a tendency to ultimately become like that which we imagine or image ourselves as being. If we image ourselves as failing we are more likely to fail. If we imagine ourselves as succeeding in some task there is a greater likelihood that we will succeed. Images that we hold onto and reinforce eventually seep into the unconscious part of our minds.

Vincent Collins describes the process in this way:

Imagination is to the emotions what illustrations are to a text, what music is to a ballad. It is the ability to form mental pictures, to visualize irritating or fearful situations in concrete form. As soon as we perceive a feeling and begin to think about it, the imagination goes to work. The imagination reinforces the thoughts, the thoughts intensify the feelings, and the whole business builds up.[1]

Another author, Alexander Whyte, says of the imagination:

It makes us full of eyes, without and within. The imagination is far stronger than any other power which we possess, and the psychologists tell us that on occasions, when the will and the imagination are in conflict, the imagination always wins. How important therefore that we should vow by the Savior's help never to throw the wrong kind of pictures on this screen in our minds, for the imagination literally has the power of making the things we picture real and effective.[2]

Why is there so much chaos today in the world, within nations, and within individuals? It is because sin is so often manifested in the wrong use of our imagination and thought life.

The first time the word *imagination* is used in Scripture it is depicted as evil: "The Lord saw that the wickedness of man was great in the earth, and that every imagination of the thoughts of his heart was only evil continually" (Gen. 6:5 *Amplified*). Paul writes, "Now this I affirm . . . that you must no longer live as the Gentiles do, in the futility of their minds" (Eph. 4:17). In Romans 1:21, he again makes reference to the negative aspects of the imagination: ". . . they became futile in their thinking and their senseless minds were darkened." Our imagination was damaged in the Fall and because of that it can be distorted and misused.

What do we suggest to our counselees then? Are they to repress their negative thoughts and imaginations, ignore them, or try to get rid of them entirely? Some people try to hide their imaginations or thoughts from God, but that is an exercise in futility. He already knows what we are thinking. Listen to the Word of God:

And thus, Solomon, my son, know thou the God of thy father, and serve him with a perfect heart and with a willing mind; for the Lord searcheth all hearts, and understandeth all the imaginations of the thoughts. If thou seek him, he will be found of thee; but if thou forsake him, he will cast thee off forever (1 Chron. 28:9 KJV).

God knows what we think, but he waits for us to take the step of transparent honesty by telling him what we are thinking. That is an indication of both our trust and our dependence upon him. As we encourage our counselees to be fully open before God, we are leading them a step closer to healing.

God knew that we would struggle with our thought lives and I believe that is why we find so many guidelines in the Bible to assist us. Think how you could help your counselees practice and incorporate these verses into their lives.

"You will guard him and keep him in perfect and constant peace whose mind [both its inclination and its character] is stayed on you . . ." (Isa. 26:3 *Amplified*).

"Be renewed in the spirit of your minds" (Eph. 4:23).

". . . Be transformed by the renewal of your mind" (Rom. 12:2).

"Finally, brethren, whatever is true, whatever is honorable, whatever is just, whatever is pure, whatever is lovely, whatever is gracious, if there be any excellence, if there is anything worthy of praise, think about these things" (Phil. 4:8).

"Gird up your minds" (1 Pet. 1:13).

"Casting down imagination . . ." (2 Cor. 10:5 KJV).

How Is Imagery Used?

How is imagery and visualization used today? In many ways.

It is used in sports for one thing. Alan Richardson, an Australian psychologist, describes the effects of visualization and imagery on the free throw scores of basketball players. Three groups of students were chosen at random, none of whom had ever practiced imagery for their playing. The first group practiced making free throws every day for twenty days. The second group of students made free throws on the first and twentieth days, with no practice in-between. The last group also practiced free throws on the first and last days, but in addition they spent twenty minutes a day imagining sinking baskets. In their minds, if they missed a shot, they tried to correct their aim on the next shot.

The first group, who practiced free throws each day, improved 24 percent between the first and last day. The second group, who only practiced on the first and last days, made no improvement. The third group, who visualized shooting free throws, improved 23 percent. Numerous studies involving dart throwing and other sporting activities show the same type of results.[3]

Jack Nicklaus has estimated that the mental image is 50 percent of his golf game. He images where he wants the ball to finish and then images the trajectory and shape of the ball during the shot.[4]

The Swiss began using imagery in coaching their Olympic skiing team in 1968 and this change in their training procedures helped them win three medals that year and additional medals in 1972. Jean Claude Killy of France, who won three Olympic gold medals in 1968, also employed imagery.[5]

Imagery is used extensively within the medical profession for the healing of disease. Some people are able to use this process to bring about dramatic changes in their bodies.

The use of relaxation techniques and imagery has become one of the most effective methods of treatment for chronic pain. Headaches, low back pain, and even chest pains have been effectively reduced with this method. A patient with arthritis is asked to visualize her joints, seeing the irritation and granules on their surfaces. She then visualizes the white blood cells coming in, picking up the granules and smoothing over the rough surfaces. An ulcer patient visualizes his stomach with the pockets in the lining, and the soreness. In his mind he visualizes the soothing effect of the medicine and of his diet, and then images the healthy cells multiplying and the white cells doing their cleansing work. He visualizes life becoming free from pain.

Individuals with high blood pressure use this technique as well, practicing both relaxation exercises and imagery. They see their blood vessels as pipes; they visualize their muscles tightening, constricting the pipes, so the blood has more difficulty getting through. Then they see the medication relaxing the muscles so the heart has an easier time pumping the blood through these vessels.[6]

This approach may sound foreign to many people and yet, medically, there is evidence that it can be beneficial. The alleviation of symptoms and the acceleration of the healing process through imagery is well substantiated in literature. Using imagery to control bleeding for both dental and surgical patients, both in preoperative and postoperative situations, is not uncommon. Hospice workers and nurses use imagery extensively for comfort and symptom control of the terminally ill individual. When one begins studying the literature and the reports from extensive research in this field, one is amazed at its effectiveness! [7]

Imagery has formed a part of the practice of some religions for hundreds of years. It is true that cults employ it sometimes and that it is misused. But the same could be said of prayer and of the Bible! The abuse of a thing should not stop us from the use of a God-given means, which I take imagery to be. It can help both counselor and counselee draw closer to the Lord when used with prayer and the sensitive leading of the Holy Spirit.

How then, can imagery be used in your counseling? Don't you need specialized training and studies in this area? No, not if you use some very simple and positive approaches. In essence, what you are doing is taking the energy a counselee has been using in a negative and nonbiblical manner and redirecting that energy into conformity with the scriptural perspective of balanced, objective, healthy imaging.

The use of self-talk or healthy inner conversations is very effective in and of itself. But it is even more effective when reinforced with two additional elements: imagery and prayer.

Seeing the Situation

As your counselees discuss with you the content of their inner conversations, ask them what images they experience as they make these statements. Some individuals just make the statements to themselves whereas others see the situation in their minds. I feel that when they actually see it the experience is stronger. For some who say they don't visualize the experience, the visualization may be so deep they are not consciously aware of it. Ask the nonvisualizing person what it would be like if he were to have an image of the situation. This helps him become more aware of what is happening in his life.

As you become more knowledgeable of your counselees' imagery tendencies, you can help them not only make accurate and objective statements but also create a healthy mental image of themselves. For example, ask the counselee, "What is another way of looking at this situation?" After he has responded, ask him to actually image or visualize it. During the week have him practice creating the mental images. As he describes a fearful future situation, ask him to image himself responding in a positive manner. Have him practice this two or three times, and then ask, "How did that feel to you as you rehearsed it in your mind?" You will probably receive a positive response. By practicing healthy imagery in your office the counselee will be more apt to practice it on his own.

Look at the thought-switching exercise suggested by Dr. Lloyd Homme concerning the fear of elevators which is described in detail in Appendix 1 (p. 188). While the person is proceeding through the steps describing his fear, ask him to create a visual image of each step during the negative process. Then ask him to describe his emotional and bodily responses to each step. As he works through the healthy steps, ask for the same responses. He will probably experience a noticeable change which can be a great source of encouragement.

Perhaps a female counselee is sharing with you her concern over a future overwhelming situation. As she anticipates its occurence, she imagines the worst, naturally. She accentuates the difficulties and rarely sees a positive solution. As you talk with her about alternate ways of responding and viewing the situation, you could lead her through an imagery exercise.

First of all, lead in prayer asking for the guidance of the Holy Spirit and for clarity and strength. Then ask the individual to close her eyes and begin to visualize herself actually facing the overwhelming situation, but facing it with Jesus Christ standing next to her. This could be a visual image or just a sense of his presence. Encourage her, in her mind, to see Jesus taking one step forward and then to see herself taking one step forward to bring herself up to Jesus. He takes another step and she moves up beside him. As she visualizes herself going through the difficult situation, she senses that Jesus is there with her actually going before her each time to strengthen her. (In doing this, we don't try to "conjure up" Christ. We sense his presence, by faith.) As the counselee saturates her mind by imaging the presence of God, she can be freed from the fear of failure or of not being able to handle whatever occurs. This is actually practicing the scriptural command to "gird up your minds" (1 Pet. 1:13). To gird means "mental exertion."

Have her visualize the experience twice, once succeeding and the other time not succeeding, but being able to handle the outcome because Christ is there with her. I find it unrealistic in some situations to always naïvely believe that the outcome will be the way we want it. God's ways and timing are different than our own. We don't always know the outcome, but failures can be handled when we realize that Jesus Christ is present with us.

Another example of using imagery is to have a person indicate a troublesome situation that generates some type of emotional response.

One counselee shared that making mistakes created three different emotional responses: anxiety, depression, and anger. And this tended to happen more than once each day. The procedure to follow in such cases is to have the person close his eyes and begin to imagine such a situation happening. Have him experience it and see it as clearly as possible. Encourage him to "see" the colors and shapes, to "hear" the sounds, and to notice as many details as possible. Then ask him to picture himself making several of his negative and self-defeating statements to himself. Encourage him to picture the situation until he begins to feel the negative emotion. When he does, have him raise his hand. Now ask him to begin imagining the worst possible consequences of his unhealthy thoughts. My counselee said, "If I continue to believe that mistakes are so awful, I'll freeze up every time. I won't be able to function at work. I could lose my job. Friends will turn me off. And the more uptight I get, the worse it will be." He did this for about thirty seconds and then stopped.

Next I ask the person to think of the same difficult situation again and this time make objective, positive comments. Have him visualize handling the problem calmly, feeling good about whatever the outcome is, and handling other people's responses rationally. Once this has occurred have him raise his hand. Then ask him to imagine the best possible consequences of his positive thoughts and reactions. It may help you both to have him talk out loud. He may say something like, "Well, making mistakes isn't the end of the world. We all do this and I'm just as human as anyone else. I can take risks. It's an opportunity to trust the Lord more. In fact, I can learn through this experience because of him. I might even amaze the people around me by having a positive, upbeat attitude during this difficult time. Yeah, won't they be taken aback . . . ?" As you teach this process during the session, encourage the counselee to practice it each day.

Imagery can help the counselee identify his thoughts and the relationship of thoughts to feelings, behavior, and consequences. By using role visualization, you ask the counselee to relive a recent unpleasant situation and specify the thoughts, feelings, and actions that occur as the situation is relived. After he learns how to do this, he can recreate several past situations for you and describe each situation as though it were happening right there.

A person who feels uneasy and rejected at church social events can be asked to recreate and describe in detail some of those occasions. As each instance is relived, he can describe his thoughts, feelings, and behavior in greater detail. This helps you to identify the specific false beliefs and unhelpful behaviors that are creating the person's difficulty.

Changing False Beliefs

Another way in which imagery can be used is to help a person gradually change his false beliefs to more realistic ones. This involves imagery to the degree that the person may actually begin to feel the upsetting emotion such as anger, anxiety, or depression. Ask the counselee to sit comfortably in a chair and then give him the following instructions:

Image as vividly as you can the details of a situation in which you became upset in the past or you might become upset in the future. Perhaps it is making a mistake, or your spouse mistreating you, someone taking you for granted, or not performing as well as you feel you should. As you visualize this situation, let yourself feel your emotional response whether it be anger, depression, fear, etc. Get in touch with this upsetting feeling as much as possible. (Give the person ten to twenty seconds to do this.) Now, force yourself to change this feeling to one of disappointment, regret, annoyance or irritation, so that you feel displeased but not upset. (Again allow ten to twenty seconds.)

Now, I would like you to consider what you just did with your thinking to cause this new feeling to occur. Try to figure out what changes you made in your thinking process to help you feel displeased but not upset. What were they? (Allow time to think.)

Open your eyes now and let's consider the new thoughts which you created to make you feel displeased, but not upset.[8]

As you talk with the person, be sure to ask for specifics. In time an individual can learn the relationship between his thoughts and his behavior and how to use imagery in a helpful manner. Once he has identified the new pattern of thinking, this could become the object for some specific prayer by the two of you on his behalf. He could ask God to quickly remind him of the new pattern of thinking, if he should fall back into the false belief pattern. He could also thank God in advance for how he is going to assist him in making this transition.

Another imagery exercise is called Visual Behavioral Rehearsal (VBR). It is usually used to help an individual perform some type of behavior that was previously avoided because of fear. The counselee is asked to select a quiet place at home, engage in some relaxation exercises, and then imagine performing the desired behavior—but on a graduated basis. (Relaxation exercises are for the purpose of relieving tension from the muscles and helping eliminate stress. See my discussion of this in Appendix 1, p. 191.) As soon as some tension or anxiety is experienced, the counselee stops the imagination process, visualizes a relaxing scene and concentrates on relaxing. When the tension and anxiety are gone, the visual behavioral rehearsal is started again. The individual continues with this process until tension increases again and another pause is necessary, or until the entire sequence of new behaviors has been imagined.

When all of the feared or anxiety-producing behaviors have been visualized without any tension or anxiety, the individual begins the VBR process in the presence of the feared situation. First of all, he completes step one of the behavioral sequence in his imagination and then in reality. If there is no anxiety or tension, begin step two, first in imagery and then in reality. The process is continued until the entire sequence of behaviors is completed with no anxiety.[9]

Approaches such as the above can be very effective when Jesus Christ is seen as part of the imagery and as being present with his support and strength.

THE HEALING OF MEMORIES

We have heard considerable discussion for the past decade over an approach called the healing of memories. Various books and articles have been written describing it and some of the suggestions sound very good, others make one wonder. A man whom I respect and consider experienced in this approach is Dr. David Seamands. In his book, *The Healing of Memories,* he discusses the use of imaging in connection with the healing of memories that plague a person. He suggests that Jesus Christ is the Lord of both time and healing. The Holy Spirit is our present and available helper.

Through the use of imagination, the counselee endeavors to recreate the painful memory and actually visualize it as it once took place. Then he prays, asking God for the kind of help he needed in that situation. A child or teenager might ask God to heal her of a terrifying or damaging experience that has emotionally crippled her.

In our minds we can walk back in time with Christ in order to minister to the hurting person. This does not change the event that occurred, but God can release the hurt and the damage. David Seamands says,

> Because we are bound by time and space, we say Christ "walks back into time" in order to minister to some hurting person. Because of our finite limitations, we do not understand *how* He does this, but we can certainly *visualize Him doing it.* Indeed, on the basis of Scripture, we have every right to picture Him as *here* and *now.*
>
> But is all this mere autosuggestion? A sort of self-hypnosis where we "psych" ourselves out by the use of mental pictures and strong imagination? No. The promises regarding the work of the Holy Spirit's participating presence and power assure us He really is here. It is the Holy Spirit who makes the transcendent Christ immediately immanent. The Spirit assures us He is truly alongside us.[10]

Using Imagery to Overcome Resentments

I would suggest that you read more about this particular approach before you make any decision or judgment concerning its use. I have found the use of imagery in counseling to be very effective in many situations, one of which is the relinquishing of resentments and the discovering of how to forgive another individual. The following suggestion is an approach that incorporates several techniques currently practiced by many therapists and ministers.

Often, counselees whom you will see will have resentments toward current family members or toward someone in their past who may even be deceased at this time. But this approach can be effective whether the person is still living or has died. Have your counselee proceed through the following steps.

First of all, have him list all the resentments that he has toward the particular person whom he has not forgiven. Each hurt or pain should be listed in as much detail as possible. Ask him to write out exactly what happened and how he felt then and feels now.

Some counselees have shared memories such as these:

—"Back then I felt hurt and rejected when you made sarcastic remarks about me in front of others and I feel angry and hindered in my relationship with you at the present time."

—"When you don't listen to me, I feel like trash and resent you terribly. Now, I don't even want to come to your house anymore."

—"I was shocked and hurt and mad when I found out you were seeing another woman. I wanted to make you pay then and I feel the same way today."

—"It wasn't fair how you treated me and my brother. We never felt accepted. And because of that I don't feel accepted by you nor anyone else today. I really feel depressed."

Be sure to let the counselee know that he may experience considerable emotional upheaval as he makes his list. Old, buried feelings may surface causing him to feel quite upset for a while. Before you have him begin his writing, ask him to pray and thank God for allowing him to wade through and expel these feelings. Have him ask God to reveal to him the hidden thoughts and feelings that have been buried for so long. Suggest that he see Jesus Christ in the room with him, smiling and giving his approval of what he is doing. Hear him say, "I want you to be cleansed and free. No longer do you have to be lame, blind, or deaf because of what happened to you."

After writing for a while, suggest that the person rest a bit as this may help other memories to emerge. This list should not be shown to anyone.

After he has finished writing, have him go into a room with two chairs and sit down. He should then close his eyes and imagine the other person sitting in the chair opposite him. As he does this, he should imagine the door opening. Jesus walks into the room, comes over, and looks at both of them and smiles. He then puts his hand on their shoulders, bridging the gap between them. Then the counselee is to open his eyes, look at the chair opposite him, and begin reading the list aloud as though the other person were actually there. Prepare the counselee for the fact that he may feel embarrassed or awkward, but those feelings will pass. After the list has been read, suggest that he sit back, relax, and imagine the other person responding in a positive manner. Imagine the person saying, "I want to hear what you have to share with me, and I will accept it. Please go ahead and tell me. I need to hear what you have to say."

Then the counselee should imagine the person he resents actually sitting there listening, hearing, nodding his head and understanding his feelings. Warn the counselee that he may experience a wide range of feelings during this time. Suggest that he share with the individual how he is feeling at this time. Remind him that not only is the other person giving him permission to share all of his present and past feelings, but Jesus is there giving him permission as well. Some counselees find that sharing just one resentment is all they can handle at one time. Others may be able to proceed through the entire list.

Before the counselee concludes his time of sharing, he needs to close his eyes again and visualize the original scene of Jesus with his hand on both his and the other person. Several minutes should be spent visualizing this. Some say they visualize the other person verbally accepting what has been said. Others say they really don't believe the other person would ever accept it, but they visualize Jesus lifting the burden of resentment from their own shoulders and they experience freedom. Some counselees may need to repeat this process several times, whereas for others a one-time experience brings about the forgiveness they needed to give and receive.

In counseling that focuses upon a person's thought life, imagery clarifies problems. The distortion of reality in the counselee's image can offer a clue as to the reason for an inappropriate reaction. It may be helpful to ask some of the following questions in order to discover the images that are accompanying the counselee's thinking.

"Do you see a picture as you're talking?"

"Would you please describe it?"

"Is it in color?"

"Is there sound?"

"Are you moving?"

"Is anyone else moving?"

"Do you smell anything?"

"Do you feel anything?"

"Is it like a movie image?"

"Is there a lot of emotional activity?" [11]

Numerous techniques can be used to modify images. If you have never been aware of or used them, at first you may consider them a bit different or even strange. But they have been tested and discovered effective. Here are several suggestions.

1. *Turn-off technique.* This approach is effective with those who have experienced some type of traumatic event or recent crisis. Often the individual relives the event for some time which tends to continue the stress and pain. It is important to get a verbal statement from the person that he or she does indeed want to relinquish this repetitious reliving of the event. Either ask the person to pray for the Lord's strength in accomplishing this task or lead in prayer yourself. Be careful to emphasize that God will be assisting in removing this painful rehearsal from the person's life.

Ask the counselee for his ideas as to how he can interrupt his fantasy. He may have some helpful suggestions or may not be able to suggest anything. You could suggest that as soon as he finds himself engaging in this fantasy he can clap his hands twice to interrupt the process. A helpful way to teach this approach is to ask him to close his eyes and begin his fantasy of the trauma. Ask him to share it aloud and as he does clap your hands twice loudly. Ask him how he felt about your hand clap. Then ask him to repeat the process and this time clap his own hands.

As soon as the negative fantasy is interrupted, have the person substitute some type of a positive imagery. This could be an image of a pleasant experience from the past or an anticipated future event. Another variation is to read to the individual one of the psalms which describes a peaceful setting and ask him to visualize or image what is being described. Ask for his response afterwards and suggest that for his substitute image he could read this psalm verse by verse, stopping between each verse, to image what is being described.

2. *Extreme images.* Sometimes individuals have difficulty with thought stoppage techniques. In such a case, when the fearful fantasy can be made more extreme, it may be helpful to have the person state the most extreme consequence of

the fantasy. By doing this he is able to consider the imagined fear in a more rational manner, which tends to relieve the fear. Often the counselee is reluctant to consider the worst consequence because he feels his anxiety and tension will increase. But even though it may initially, he will be surprised to find that it diminishes and he actually feels better.

Sometimes the person is afraid to consider the consequences out of fear that this will bring them on. And again he discovers it has just the opposite effect. The purpose of this approach is to help him see if he can learn to accept and tolerate the experience he fears. Once he is able to face the situation to its fullest, help him create an image of either being successful in the experience or being able to handle whatever comes.

A young seminary student, in anticipation of preaching his third sermon in his home church, had created a terrible state of anxiety for himself by mentally rehearsing the worst. I suggested that if he wanted to imagine a disaster occurring, that he needed some assistance from someone such as myself. I suggested several additional negative and even worse possibilities and asked him to imagine these in his fantasy. He did this, but it was interesting that he stopped himself in the middle of one and said, "This is ridiculous. You know what the possibilities of this occurring are? There is no way that this would happen."

I replied, "What are the possibilities of the others happening then? You can go ahead and choose to fantasize in this way, or you could use the same energy to help yourself have a greater chance of doing the type of job I think you really want to do. Which would you prefer?" He realized that he had a choice and began to use his imagination in a positive manner.

One of the most helpful approaches to use is having the person imagine going through the fearful experience with Jesus alongside. Often before imagining this, it is helpful to read several passages of Scripture which emphasize that we are not alone and that Jesus Christ is with us in all experiences of life. So many of us know this intellectually, but experientially it is lacking.

3. *Future imagery.* This approach can be used with individuals who are either concerned about the future or who are

a bit stuck as to the direction in which they want to proceed in life. Ask the person to select a date three months in the future. Then ask him to imagine what he would like to have happen by that time. Ask him to imagine getting up and going through the day with his new attitudes and behaviors and have him indicate what areas went easily and which ones were difficult or that he avoided. Then interview him as though both of you were actually there three months from this time. Ask him what has been accomplished, how he views his problems, and how some of his former beliefs have been changed. Ask what specific Scriptures have come alive in his life and why they did.

The goals the counselee selects should be attainable and realistic. If he should choose unrealistic goals or ones that involve changing other individuals, you can discuss how his expectations are setting him up to experience failure.

After realistic goals are established through this imagery, your task will be to help him develop a plan to reach his goals. Part of the planning will be having him use imagery to visualize how he will spend the day three months from this time. This imagery should be practiced daily and you should encourage him to develop the feelings that are associated with these final goals. Be sure to emphasize that part of the effectiveness of this approach is repetition. The more it is practiced, the greater the interest in attaining the goal.[12]

IS SELF-TALK THE ANSWER?

Is self-control of negative self-talk and negative inner conversations, along with imagery, the answer to changing wrong patterns of thinking? Yes and no. By itself, no. It is a means or a tool. Without assistance, none of us has the capability to extract the negative thoughts and images from our minds. Colossians 3:15 states, "And let the peace of Christ rule in your hearts. . . ." The person of Jesus Christ is the answer. Jesus himself wants both us and our counselees to be open about our thought life and the inner images that are there. All aberrant thoughts should be brought to Christ. By sharing them with him and asking him for strength through the ministry of the Holy Spirit, change will occur.

As you work with your counselee, find out if he really deeply desires to change. Desire or motivation is essential if change is to occur. Each one must come to the place of being able to say, "God, I do not want to have the kind of thought life I have been having. I want to be rid of the negative images. They have created a barrier between me and others and between me and you. I want the thoughts and images you have for me. Help me to use my imagination and thought life in such a way that I can grow, mature, help others more, and bring glory to you!"

Ask the counselee to pray for the desire to be rid of the old pattern of thinking. Suggest that he invite Jesus Christ into his thought life and allow the Holy Spirit into the depths of his imagination, to bring to light any images or thoughts that are creating a barrier. It is safe to do this in the presence of Jesus Christ and with His strength and comfort. During this prayer time, when a troublesome thought or image comes to mind, encourage the counselee to see himself taking it in his hands and giving it to Jesus.

Some people have found it helpful as they pray to lift one hand to the head, place the thought in that hand, and then reach forward and place it in Jesus' outstretched hands. The physical movement, along with the prayer, has a greater sense of reality to it and strengthens their motivation. This type of praying takes time and often needs to be repeated, for each image or thought that emerges. This is not to say that these thoughts will never return, but now the person will be able to confront them in a new way. It was Martin Luther who said we can't stop the birds from flying over our heads, but we can stop them from building a nest in our hair.

This approach, aligned with the reworking of self-talk and the use of prayer can bring about what Isaiah has assured us: "Thou dost keep him in perfect peace, whose mind is stayed on thee" (Isaiah 26:3).

Guide your counselees to ask God for clearness of thought and direction. Encourage them to use their God-given power of imagination to bring about change in their own lives and to bring glory to him.

CHAPTER SEVEN

THE UNTAPPED RESOURCE OF COUNSELING—PRAYER

WITH THE RING of the phone one morning I found myself speaking to a 32-year-old man who was concerned about his forthcoming marriage. As we talked he told me he wanted to marry this lovely woman he had been going with for over a year. He had made a commitment and given her the ring; but fears stemming from his childhood had begun to emerge. (This is a not uncommon situation.)

We continued to talk about the marriage and the normal concerns that most individuals have concerning this major life step. "I feel I need prayer at this time," he concluded. "Would you seal our conversation with prayer?" And at that moment, distanced by many miles, yet very close because of the modern convenience of phone lines and our common relationship of Jesus Christ, I prayed for him. I asked for God's insight, direction, clarity of thought and leading, and peace to invade this brother's life.

We do not have to be face to face to minister in prayer. As we minister over the phone to those who are close to us, or to strangers, our prayer draws them closer to relying upon the Lord instead of upon themselves or us.

As I get to know counselees in my office, I share with them during the first or second session that, as part of my counseling ministry, I will pray for them each day. And I tell them I would appreciate their sharing with me from time to time what they would like me to pray about in their lives so that I can be sure to be current. Many of them are taken aback that someone would remember them in prayer. But over the years many counselees have said that what kept them going was knowing that one person was praying for them.

I admit that there are those days when I do not pray as I have promised that I would. But I think that 90 percent of the time I am consistent in this practice.

Praying accomplishes several things. It releases the person to God and it reminds us that we are not the one who is the final resource in his life. We need the direct intervention of God in the life of the person to guide, sustain, and comfort him. I have discovered that by keeping a list and praying for my counselees' specific concerns and issues, when they walk into my office I know what their concerns have been the week before. Praying is a reminder and reinforces their situation upon my mind.

Sometimes the counselee asks, "How did you remember what we discussed? I don't see you ever taking many notes?" My answer is that praying is a reminder.

No law says that each session must be opened or closed in prayer. There will be occasions when, in the middle of a session, you need to pray for the hurt and pain of an individual. There will be times when you are stumped, as I have been, and you won't know how to proceed or what to say. It is perfectly all right to admit that: "I'm not sure where to go next or what is more pressing. Let's just stop and I would like to ask God for guidance and insight for the direction needed at this time."

One minister shared his experience of praying during the middle of a session. He had been counseling with a woman who had been sexually abused and was very suicidal. Since he felt blocked in discovering the core problem, as the woman had not yet shared some of her past life, the minister stopped to pray. He asked the Lord to help him discover the deepest wound of her life, which was the basis for her depression and despair, and as he prayed the number sixteen came to his mind. He asked her if something had happened in her sixteenth year and she was quite surprised. Looking at him with amazement, she said, "That was the year my father raped me." Once this was revealed, they could deal with the basic problem.

Another way of praying is for the counselor to look over the schedule of those whom he or she will be seeing on that day and to set aside a few minutes of quiet time in the office. The counselor should visualize each person walking into the office and sitting down. Pray specifically for the person's needs, for a listening ear and a sensitivity toward the person, and for the presence of Jesus Christ there in your office.

Some counselors reserve a few minutes between sessions in order to pray in this manner for the next person they are to see during the day. Others have set aside a small office nearby just for prayer and meditation for the counselee. They suggest that the counselee arrive a few minutes early and sit in the room relaxing and praying for the counseling session.

The importance of the power of God working in our lives and in the counselee's life cannot be overestimated. I remember an experience that happened not long ago. A woman in her fifties had been in counseling for several months. She came in quite depressed and told of numerous incidents in her childhood and adolescence that had left her with emotional wounds. She struggled with low self-esteem and tremendous feelings of inferiority. Her self-talk was negative and she had many false beliefs about herself, her own ability, what she thought others thought and felt about her, and about God's perspective of her. In each session I attempted to bring some balance into these thoughts and perspectives that she had reinforced for so many years. And each month there appeared to be some improvement.

But as it is with so many who struggle with negative self-talk, her negative filter even affected her memories of the past. As others do, she tended to recall the bad that occurred in her life and often could not even recall the positive experiences.

One of her wounds concerned a harsh, demanding father. She said that she never had been accepted by him and never had heard him tell her he loved her or cared for her. She grew up feeling as though she were the black sheep of the family.

One day when she arrived for her session she reported the following incident to me:

> You will never guess what happened to me the other night. We had a pleasant evening with our grown children and then went to bed. We went to sleep and then about 2:30 I woke up and was wide awake. I decided to pray and asked Jesus to be present with me and let me know that he was there. And you know what? It was as though he came into the room, pulled up a chair and sat there talking with me. I continued to talk with him and the most amazing thing happened. As I conversed with him, he brought to my mind one incident after another that I had totally forgotten.

And in an excited manner she recounted several forgotten incidents in which her father *had* shown care and love for her as well as a time when she asked her father why he had never loved her. He told her that he and her mother had always loved and cherished her; they just were not people who talked about it that much. She told me that she prayed for over two hours allowing Jesus to free up her memories to recall times of love and acceptance.

As she described what had occurred, I could actually see changes in her, in the way she talked, and in her expression. It was a deep spiritual blessing for me as the counselor to see how God worked in her life. We had much more work to do in counseling, but both of us had a greater sense of the presence of Jesus Christ working in her life.

I learned an important lesson in this experience as well. Many of our counselees have blockages in their lives as well as distorted and unbalanced memories. We need to call upon God to break down the walls and bring balance into their lives. During the counseling session, you may want to stop and pray and ask the counselee to visualize the presence of Jesus in the room right at the moment, removing the barriers so that a balanced remembering may occur.

The core of counseling is prayer. But too little is said about prayer in counseling and too little is written about its use during the session and between sessions. This is not a chapter on what prayer is or how to pray according to this pattern or that pattern. There are numerous books written on those topics. What I want to address is the usage of prayer as a means of healing in the process of counseling.

Prayer is not something just to tack on at the end of a counseling session to make it "Christian" counseling. Prayer reflects a dependency upon God that brings us back again to the matter of attitude. We as ministers or counselors can be more effective if we remind ourselves at the beginning of a day or the beginning of each session that *God* is the one who will effect change and healing within the session. Such an attitude will make a difference in your counseling.

SELECTIONS FROM THE BIBLE

We pray because it is our privilege and a means of communication with God the Father. We pray because the Word of God instructs us to pray. Consider with me some passages from the Word of God regarding our own prayer life as well as that of those we counsel.

As we pray, we know that we are welcomed into God's presence. (Hebrews 4:16, "Let us then with confidence draw near to the throne of grace, that we may receive mercy and find grace to help in time of need." Psalm 66:20, "Blessed be God, because he has not rejected my prayer or removed his steadfast love from me!")

When we pray, we can call upon the Holy Spirit to guide our prayers. (Romans 8:26, 27, "The Spirit helps us in our weakness; for we do not know how to pray as we ought, but the Spirit himself intercedes for us with sighs too deep for words. And he who searches the hearts of men knows what is the mind of the Spirit, because the Spirit intercedes for the saints according to the will of God." Ephesians 6:18, "Pray at all times in the Spirit, with all prayers and supplication.")

When we pray, we do so with confession, praise, and thanksgiving. (1 John 1:9, "If we confess our sins, he is faithful and just, and will forgive our sins and cleanse us from all unrighteousness." Ephesians 1:3, "Blessed be the God and Father of our Lord Jesus Christ, who has blessed us in Christ with every spiritual blessing in the heavenly places." Ephesians 5:20, "Always and for everything giving thanks in the name of our Lord Jesus Christ. . . ." Psalm 118:1, "O give thanks to the Lord, for he is good; his steadfast love endures forever!")

One of the important principles of prayer is to rely upon the promises of God. (Matthew 7:7, "Ask, and it will be given you; seek, and you will find; knock, and it will be opened to you." 1 Peter 3:12, "For the eyes of the Lord are upon the righteous, and his ears are open to their prayer. . . ." 1 John 5:14, 15. ". . . if we ask anything according to his will he hears us. And if we know that he hears us in whatever we ask, we know that we have obtained the requests made of him." Psalm 4:3, "But know that the Lord has set apart the godly for himself; the Lord hears when I call to him.")

We can read a number of Bible passages in session with the counselee to discover the truth of God's Word and to use as a model for prayer right at that time.

For those who are fearful: Psalm 56:3–4, "When I am afraid, I put my trust in thee. In God, whose word I praise, in God I trust without a fear. What can flesh do to me?"

For those who are suffering: 1 Peter 1:3, 6, 7, "Blessed be the God and Father of our Lord Jesus Christ! By his great mercy we have been born anew to a living hope . . . In this you rejoice, though now for a little while you may have to suffer various trials, so that the genuineness of your faith, more precious than gold which though perishable is tested by fire, may redound to praise and glory. . . ." 1 Peter 4:12, 13, ". . . do not be surprised at the fiery ordeal which comes upon you to prove you, . . . But rejoice in so far as you share Christ's sufferings, that you may also rejoice and be glad when his glory is revealed." James 1:2, 3, "Count it all joy, my brethren, when you meet various trials, for you know that the testing of your faith produces steadfastness."

For those who are worried: Philippians 4:6–9, "Have no anxiety about anything, but in everything by prayer and supplication with thanksgiving let your requests be made known to God. And the peace of God, which passes all understanding will keep your hearts and your minds in Christ Jesus. Finally, brethren, whatever is true, whatever is honorable, whatever is just, whatever is pure, whatever is lovely, whatever is gracious, if there is any excellence, if there is anything worthy of praise, think about these things. What you have learned and received and heard and seen in me, do; and the God of peace will be with you." Psalm 37:1, "Fret not because of the wicked, be not envious of wrongdoers!"

For those who feel oppressed and in distress: Psalm 4:1, "Answer me when I call, O God of my right! Thou hast given me room when I was in distress. Be gracious to me and hear my prayer." Psalm 55:4–8, 16–18, "My heart is in anguish within me, the terrors of death have fallen upon me. Fear and trembling come upon me, and horror overwhelms me. And I say, 'O that I had wings like a dove! I would fly away and be at rest, yea, I would wander afar, I would lodge in the wilderness, I would haste to find me a shelter from the raging wind and tempest.' But I call upon God; and the Lord will save me. Evening and morning and at noon I utter my complaint and moan, and he will hear my voice. He will deliver my soul in safety from the battle that I wage, for many are arrayed against me." Psalm 77:2–6, 11, 12, "In the day of my trouble I seek the Lord; in the night my hand is stretched out without wearying; my soul refuses to be comforted. I think of God, and I moan; I meditate, and my spirit faints. Thou dost hold my eyelids from closing; I am so troubled that I cannot speak. I consider the days of old, I remember the years long ago. I commune with my heart in the night; I meditate and search my spirit: . . . I will call to mind the deeds of the Lord; yea, I will remember thy wonders of old. I will meditate on all thy works, and muse on thy mighty deeds." Isaiah 43:1–3, " 'Fear not, for I have redeemed you; I have called you by name, you are mine. When you pass through the waters I will be with you; and through the rivers, they shall not overwhelm you; when you walk through fire you shall not be burned, and the flame shall not consume you. For I am the Lord your God, the Holy One of Israel, your Savior.' "

For those who need God's forgiveness: Micah 7:18, 19, "Who is a God like thee, pardoning iniquity and passing over transgression for the remnant of his inheritance? He does not retain his anger for ever because he delights in steadfast love. He will again have compassion upon us, he will tread our iniquities under foot. Thou wilt cast all our sins into the depths of the sea." Psalm 32:5, "I acknowledged my sin to thee, and I did not hide my iniquity; I said, 'I will confess my transgressions to the Lord'; then thou didst forgive the guilt of my sin."

THE USE OF DEVOTIONAL MATERIAL

One of the means available to assist counselees in developing their own prayer life apart from the counseling environment is encouraging them to use devotional material, particularly the reading of prayers. For several years I have used a little book, *A Diary of Private Prayer,* by John Baillie. First published in 1936, it has had repeated printings and has been used throughout the world. Such books are not to take the place of our own personally constructed prayers. However, reading a prayer aloud in a quiet place and meditating upon the words of the prayer is a very meaningful experience for many people.

Listed here are samples of a morning prayer and an evening prayer.

MORNING

Almighty God, who art ever present in the world without me, in my spirit within me, and in the unseen world above me, let me carry with me through this day's life a most real sense of Thy power and Thy glory.

O God without me, forbid that I should look today upon the work of Thy hands and give no thought to Thee the Maker. Let the heavens declare Thy glory to me and the hills Thy majesty. Let every fleeting loveliness I see speak to me of a loveliness that does not fade. Let the beauty of earth be to me a sacrament of the beauty of holiness made manifest in Jesus Christ my Lord.

O God within me, give me grace today to recognize the stirrings of Thy Spirit within my soul and to listen most attentively to all that Thou hast to say to me. Let not the noises of the world ever so confuse me that I cannot hear Thee speak. Suffer me never to deceive myself as to the meaning of Thy commands; and so let me in all things obey Thy will, through the grace of Jesus Christ my Lord.

O God above me, God who dwellest in light unapproachable, teach me, I beseech Thee, that even my highest thoughts of Thee are but dim and distant shadowings of Thy transcendent glory. Teach me that if Thou art in nature, still more art Thou greater than nature. Teach me that if Thou art in my heart, still more art Thou greater than my heart. Let my soul rejoice in Thy mysterious greatness. Let me take refuge in the thought that Thou art utterly beyond me, beyond the sweep of my imagination, beyond the comprehension of my mind, Thy judgments being unsearchable and Thy ways past finding out.

O Lord, hallowed be Thy name. Amen.[1]

If you are ministering to people who struggle with worry or other aspects of their thought life, the evening prayer read aloud before turning off the light can help bring a sense of peace to an otherwise troubled mind.

EVENING

O Thou who art from everlasting to everlasting, I would turn my thoughts to Thee as the hours of darkness and of sleep begin. O Sun of my soul, I rejoice to know that all night I shall be under the unsleeping eye of One who dwells in eternal light.

To thy care, O Father, I would now commend my body and my soul. All day Thou hast watched over me and Thy companionship has filled my heart with peace. Let me not go through any part of this night unaccompanied by Thee.

Give me sound and refreshing sleep:

Give me safety from all perils:

Give me in my sleep freedom from restless dreams:

Give me control of my thoughts, if I should lie awake:

Give me wisdom to remember that the night was made for sleeping, and not for the harbouring of anxious or fretful or shameful thoughts.

Give me grace, if as I lie abed I think at all, to think upon Thee.[2]

Many of the difficulties which you encounter in counseling are present because of the counselee's misuse of his or her imagination. And yet the imagination, rightly used, can be a tool for healing. I am using the word healing here to indicate spiritual growth which can take many forms. It means drawing closer to the person of Jesus Christ and allowing the new nature or new self to progress toward "the new nature, which is being renewed in knowledge after the image of its creator" (Col. 3:10b). Healing means bringing a balance into one's emotional life and thought life and reflecting the leading and guidance of the Holy Spirit which enables this change to occur.

As you both use prayer and teach the counselee to pray, be sure to rely upon the Holy Spirit for instruction in how to pray. How is this done? Suggest to your counselee that as the two of you pray, that you call upon the Holy Spirit for insight and intuition for what you need to pray about as well as the direction to take within the counseling session. Then pause for a minute or several minutes allowing the Holy Spirit *to bring to mind through your imagination* the direction needed in prayer and counseling. Too often we quickly pray with our own words which come from our intellect. Our prayer lacks freshness because it reflects our own direction and not that of the Holy Spirit. It is as though we are uncomfortable with silence and feel that we must offer the right sounding prayer. Too often our quick words block out the words the Holy Spirit wants to say to us.

In the first chapter of this book, I suggested that we be sensitive to the style of language that a person uses and learn that person's language. Just as a person's language varies, so will the way he responds with his imagination vary from that of others. Some people's imaginations respond with concrete pictures. Others respond via moods, feelings, or sensations. Some find their imagination responding with a blending of all of these. I mention this because you will note these differences when you ask your counselee to respond and share how the Holy Spirit responded to him through his imagination.

Some counselees will say that as they prayed they *saw* Jesus responding to them and directing them in their imagination. Others will say they *sensed* his presence in the room with them even though they didn't actually see anyone. Still others will say they *felt* warm feelings inside, like when another person affirms them.

The person you are working with may respond in a different manner than you are accustomed to, but realize that God and his Holy Spirit speak to each of us in the language we understand best. You and I as counselors can adapt and allow our counselees to both experience and be spoken to in a manner different than the way the Holy Spirit ministers to us.

DIRECTED PRAYER

Since the emphasis in this book is on the imagination and thought life, I would like to relate an example of the use of directed prayer in the counselee's thought life. Helping the person refashion his pattern of thinking through various suggestions and techniques can be beneficial. Yet it can be an empty experience without the ministry of the Holy Spirit. Directed prayer is a good way to tap into the power of the Holy Spirit to change lives.

The initial step in this process is actually a step of spiritual growth. Suggest to the counselee that he consecrate his imagination to God and ask Him to help him cleanse his thought life of anything that is hindering him. As believers the Holy Spirit gives us access to the specific thoughts that need to be healed as well as to memories from our past that also need to be identified. Through a quiet time of praying, the counselee can call upon the Holy Spirit to bring to mind the specific pattern of thinking, specific emotional responses generated by his thoughts, or repressed and hidden memories that need healing. Urge the counselee to imagine himself standing in the presence of Jesus, inviting him to send his Holy Spirit into the recesses of his imagination to begin the process of an extensive inventory. Sometimes the answer comes as a picture flashed across the person's mind, or as a sentence or a sensation. Suggest that he sit and allow the Holy Spirit to bring the answer. Too often, people try to make it happen. When an answer occurs, I suggest that the person thank the Lord for bringing this to mind.

Honest sharing with God through prayer is the next important step. Too often, instead of bringing negative thoughts or images before God, we hide or repress them. If we feel any guilt or mixed feelings about our thoughts, we respond by saying to ourselves, *I shouldn't have that thought or response. I should get rid of that.* Then we endeavor to put out of our mind that thought, by our own strength. In reality, however, these things have just been put aside for a while, ready to enter again as soon as possible.

Repression of a thought involves repressing the tension that the thought produces. To be sure, that tension will appear again. Scripture teaches that we are to put away evil (or negative or harmful) thoughts and eliminate them completely (Eph. 4:31 and Col. 3:5–8). But we *cannot* do that on our own. The techniques suggested in this book will be limited in their effectiveness unless we pray honestly and invite the Holy Spirit to work in our lives.

How does this occur?

First of all by being open and honest in prayer and stating specifically the thoughts and images that occur in our minds. Sharing the thought is far better than condemning oneself for thinking it. At the same time that we admit the thought, however, one additional element needs to be present—the desire to give up the thought or thinking pattern. For some individuals, this step may seem impossible. You can help them by saying, "Let's pray for you to be willing to give that up."

Many counselees do not have that desire and it troubles some of them. They need to know that the desire comes from God himself: ". . . for God is at work in you, both to will and to work for his good pleasure" (Phil. 2:13).

As you work in this way, ask your counselee, "How do you envision God responding to your admission of your thoughts and images and patterns of thinking?"

How the counselee responds may let you know what his or her image of God is. Too often Christians have created God in their own image or someone else's image instead of seeking him as he is presented in Scripture. Many of us live with distortions of God. Some see God as a Judge or Legal God who keeps an account of what we do wrong. He just sits there waiting for a mistake. Or we see him as a policeman hiding around the corner waiting to jump out and apprehend us when we make a mistake. Or we may see him as an unpleasant taskmaster.

Our distorted views of God lead to difficulties, including the inability to feel forgiven, the inability to forgive others, difficulties in trusting and surrendering to God, and difficulties with perfectionism. So often I find terrible theological distortions because individuals have developed their own concept of God based upon their experiences and their relationship with their parents. I encourage them to read J. I. Packer's book, *Knowing God* [3] in order to help them develop a balanced and healthy concept of God. Packer's book is quite extensive and another resource that may be easier is *Your God is Too Small* by J. B. Phillips.[4] If people see God as negative, they will avoid going to him. They are afraid of being judged and rejected. Many individuals who have negative thoughts about themselves and others project the same type of thinking upon God.

I like the positive way in which Lloyd Ogilvie describes the process of going to our Lord in prayer. Instead of Christ judging us because of our distorted thoughts and behavior, and making us reveal our thoughts, he says,

What would you be like if you allowed me to form your character and personality like mine? In prayer He [God] activates our imagination to picture the person we long to be by His transforming power and then offers us the help we need. He does that by removing the barriers to Christlikeness. Most of us are haunted with fears. These shape our personalities into inverted, cautious distortions. He helps us look at these one by one. Then He deals with the memories which lurk within—the times we failed, were hurt by others, or stunted in our personality growth by the debilitating experiences during the early years of our lives. The Lord allows us to look honestly at what our parents and our families did to encourage or discourage our emergence as self-accepting, life-affirming people capable of receiving and giving love. As we probe deeper with His loving guidance in prayer, He helps us receive and give forgiveness. Memories are expunged of their poison.

Now the Lord is ready to deal with habit patterns in our attitudes. Why do we react the way we do? What causes us to respond to some people and reject others? What lack of security in His love makes us negatively critical, judgmental, or hostile?

Consistently in prayer with the Lord we can look back over the previous day and affirm progress and question the deeper causes of any lack of freedom. He gently, but persistently, touches the raw nerve of the deeper causes.[5]

Thus in prayer the initial stages are admitting that our thought life needs to be renewed and changed, envisioning Christ as willing to minister to us, and developing the desire to change, or the desire to desire the change.

During this time of prayer some counselees take each distorted or negative thought, repeat it, and give it in that way over to God. Others may almost act out the prayer by seeing themselves holding each thought in their hands and literally giving it over to Jesus Christ who accepts it in his hands and takes it away. This process of prayer is concluded by dedicating the counselee's imagination to God in a realistic manner. This means that the counselee is relinquishing ownership of his thought life and imagination to God. Few individuals actually do this because they gain a great deal of satisfaction from thoughts that do not follow the direction God would desire. A realistic prayer I once heard went like this,

> Lord, I am at the place of asking you to take over my thought life and my imagination and not only cleanse them but give me the power to control the thoughts. Oh, yeah, I know which thoughts help me and which ones create problems. But I admit I am a creature of habit and I have worked for a long time refining my negative, distorted thoughts. I want to be rid of them and I know this will take time. Help me not to panic when I fall back into the old pattern. Just gently remind me and I will respond to your prodding. I need it because I want the peace in my life which you have promised. Help me be patient with me and with you. Thank you for hearing me, accepting me and thank you for what you will be doing now and in the future.

This was a sincere and balanced prayer for change.

KEEPING A JOURNAL

Some individuals find help and growth through keeping a journal, a simple record of personal insights, prayers, significant events, reflections, and spiritual intuitions. The one writing in a journal responds to questions such as, "What were the significant thoughts and feelings of this day?" "How did I respond to them?" Then he or she writes down the answers. The act of writing something down tells the person that it is important. When an inner experience is written about or a dream recorded, the person is making a statement that this was significant. It is something that needs to be remembered.

Another way in which a journal is used is to express oneself in prayer. By writing out a prayer or even writing the prayer in the form of a letter to God, greater thought and deliberation occurs and the experience can take on tremendous meaning. Ask your counselee, "Have you ever written a letter to God?" and watch his response. Some are quite surprised but soon realize that in prayer we are communicating via a spoken or thought-out letter. Encourage the person to write one or two letters during the week or to write out one prayer and bring it in to share with you. You will learn much about his concerns, his concept of God, and his relationship with Him. I have several counselees who keep journals and on occasion we look back several weeks or months and compare what was written then and now. We discover that significant changes have taken place.

THE MOST COMMON QUESTION—"WHY GOD, WHY?"

As you counsel individuals, families, and couples, many will be in emotional, spiritual, and physical pain. Their distress level will be high. They will be in crisis and wanting to break out of their difficult situation. The most common questions coming from the lips of nonbelievers and believers alike are "Why God, why?" "When God, when will this be over?" "Will I survive?"

Often the prayer they are expressing and the way in which they want you to pray for them amounts to one thing. They want an instantaneous, magic solution. They want immediate change back to the time when they weren't sick, when they weren't getting a divorce, when they still had a job, or had not lost a parent or child.

Of course, we would all like to see the pain and stress removed and the disaster lifted. The "why" questions of life are a normal and necessary initial response to the upsets of life, and perhaps their role is to help us cope. Perhaps people hope for an answer in order to make some sense of the turmoil they are experiencing.

For thousands of years people have been asking these same questions. One of the opportunities you will have is to be able, at the proper time, to help those you counsel begin to develop a perspective on life that enables them to accept difficulties and develop a greater dependency upon God regardless of the outcome. Part of our task in counseling is to help the counselee look at life from God's perspective instead of from the view of his own desires. It is important that we allow the individual to work through his feelings and questions until he is able to consider another perspective regarding what is happening to him.

Your counselees' questions are the same as Job's—the man

who lost everything in just one day. One devastating crisis after another struck. His family, possessions, wealth, and health went. After several days of silence he began asking the same questions we and our counselees ask in times of distress:

"Why didn't I die at birth?"

"Why can't I die now?"

"Why has God done this to me?"

Job threw the question *why* at God sixteen times. Each time there was silence. And you know . . . silence was probably the best answer. I know that sounds strange, but if God had given Job the answer to his question right away, would he have accepted it? Would you? I have had counselees ask the question week after week. No answer I could give at those times would satisfy. I respond with, "I can't give you an answer. I wish I could. I just don't know at this time." Any other answer would elicit arguments and debates. But by not having the answer, we have the opportunity to learn to live by faith.

Share with your counselees some of the *whys* in Scripture. The prophet Habakkuk, for example asked a few questions in his day. He was appalled by the suffering he saw. Hear his complaint in Habakkuk 1:2–4.

> O Lord, how long shall I cry for help, and thou wilt not hear? Or cry to thee, "Violence!" and thou wilt not save? Why dost thou make me see wrongs and look upon trouble? Destruction and violence are before me; strife and contention arise. So the law is slacked and justice never goes forth. For the wicked surround the righteous, so justice goes forth perverted.

Although Habakkuk's *why* seemed to go unanswered, he eventually came to the place of confidence and hope.

> Though the fig trees do not blossom, nor fruit be on the vines, the produce of the olive fail and the fields yield no food, the flock be cut off from the fold and there be no herd in the stalls, yet I will rejoice in the Lord, I will joy in the God of my salvation (Hab. 3:17, 18).

In spite of everything falling apart, Habakkuk could rejoice in the Lord.

In counseling, we try to help the individual come to the place of confidence and hope so that he or she too can say, "In spite of . . . I will rejoice." The goal, whether the counselee realizes it or not, is not just to cope, but to celebrate no matter what!

God does not explain all suffering in the world or the meaning of each problem that occurs. There is no clear explanation for some events that take place. Therefore, we shouldn't begin to play God by giving some made up answer that may be an attempt to cover our own anxiety in not having all the answers. Our counselees' questions and their intensity in asking them can unnerve us if we let them. God may not answer the *Whys* but he does tell all of us to trust so that we can prevail in the time of trouble.

A person who was experiencing a very upsetting time of life said to me, "You know, it feels as though I opened the doors of a blast furnace and the heat I'm experiencing is unbearable. I feel as though I'm melting away. There's going to be nothing left of me."

"But If Not . . ."

Sometimes life does feel that way. However, one of the greatest principles for handling life's upsets is found in the statement of three men who literally faced the heat of a furnace. Listen to their solution.

"Is it true, O Shadrach, Meshach, and Abednego, that you do not serve my gods or worship the golden image which I have set up? Now if you are ready when you hear the sound of the horn, pipe, lyre, trigon, harp, bagpipe, and every kind of music, to fall down and worship the image which I have made, well and good; but if you do not worship, you shall immediately be cast into a burning fiery furnace; and who is the god that will deliver you out of my hands?" Shadrach, Meshach, and Abednego answered the king, "O Nebuchadnezzar, we have no need to answer you in this matter. If it be so, our God whom we serve is able to deliver us from the burning fiery furnace; and he will deliver us out of your hand, O king. But if not, be it known to you, O king, that we will not serve your gods or worship the golden image which you have set up" (Dan. 3:14–18).

There is the key statement to hold onto! *"But if not. . . ."* It is a statement of trust, of faith, and of living above and beyond the circumstances of life.

Each of us has his own dreams, desires, expectations, and hopes for his life. If these come about, it is easy to say, "Everything is all right. I can handle life and I'm content. Now I can have the peace and stability I was looking for."

For many today, faith is dependent upon getting God to do what they feel they need or want. However, this is not the biblical pattern. It's all right to say, "Oh, I hope it turns out that way." "I hope the escrow doesn't fall through." "I hope he pulls through the operation." But all of us must learn to say, "I hope . . . but even if it doesn't turn out that way, *it will be all right."*

Stability in life begins when a person can say those words: "even if He does not!" This is not a denial of life's problems. It is not rolling over and giving up or refusing to face life. It is a matter of surrendering to the wisdom of God. This gives us strength.

Each person whom you counsel in your office is facing his or her own "fiery furnace." When such intense upsets strike, the counselee must experience the normal emotional responses that are part of the healing process. Then, with God's strength and stability, he or she must face the results. God does not always send in a rescue squad to get people out of the difficulty. (He doesn't always extinguish the fire in the furnace.) He does come in and say, "Let's go through this together." Things will be better tomorrow, but better from God's perspective. Saying, "even if He doesn't" means being willing to leave the results to God.

God gives us all the grace to live life. Grace is really God's assurance that life can be all right when everything in it is all wrong. It is the power to live life today as if things will be all right tomorrow. Lewis Smedes says it so well,

> Grace does not make everything right. Grace's trick is to show us that it is right for us to live; that it is truly good, wonderful even, for us to be breathing and feeling at the same time that everything clustering around us is wholly wretched. Grace is not a ticket to Fantasy Island; Fantasy Island is dreamy fiction. Grace is not a potion to charm life to our liking; charms are magic. Grace does not cure all our concerns, transform all our kids into winners, or send us all soaring into the high skies of sex and success. Grace is rather an amazing power to look earthy reality full in the face, see its sad and tragic edges, feel its cruel cuts, join in the primeval chorus against its outrageous unfairness, and yet feel in your deepest being that it is good and right for you to be alive on God's good earth.[6]

There are many hurts, but there is a positive side also. Months or years after a difficult time, people admit the good that took place during or as a result of the situation.

The counselee's theology (and ours) will affect how he or she responds to life's difficulties? Our response to life's upsets and crises will be determined by our understanding of God. The one helps or hinders the other.

All of us tend to put faith in formulas. We feel comfortable with predictability, regularity, and assurance. We want God to be like that and so we try to create him in the image of what we want him to be and what we want him to do. However, none of us can predict what God will do. Paul reminds us of that in Roman's 11:33: "O the depth of the riches and wisdom and knowledge of God! How unsearchable are his judgments and how inscrutable his ways!"

God is not too busy elsewhere or noncaring. He is neither insensitive nor punitive. He is supreme, sovereign, loving, and sensitive.

I don't fully comprehend God. And our counselees don't

fully comprehend him either. I, too, have unanswered questions about some of the events of my life. But all of life's trials, problems, crises, and suffering occur by divine permission.

God allows us to suffer. This may be the only solution to the problem that we will ever receive. Nothing can touch the Christian without having first received the permission of God. If I do not accept that statement, then I really do not believe that God is sovereign—and if I do not believe in His sovereignty, then I am helpless before all the forces of heaven and hell.[7]

Why God Allows Suffering

God allows suffering for his purpose and for his reasons. He gives the permission. This should help counselors and counselees alike see God as the gracious controller of the universe. God is free to do as he desires, and he doesn't have to give any of us explanations nor share his reasons. He doesn't owe us. He has already given us his Son and his Holy Spirit who strengthen and guide us. We look at problems and crises and say "why?" Jesus asks us to look at them and say "why not?"

What God allows the counselee to experience is for the person's own growth. This is often difficult to both comprehend and accept, but God has arranged the seasons of nature to produce growth and he arranges the experiences of the seasons of our lives for growth also. Some days bring sunshine and some bring storms. Both are necessary. He knows the amount of pressure that any person can handle. First Corinthians 10:13 tells us he will, ". . . not let you be tempted beyond what you can bear." But he does let all of us be tempted, feel pain, and experience suffering. He gives us not always what we think we need or want, but what will produce growth. I'm sure that you, the reader, have experienced pain and growth which when sensitively timed and shared would benefit the person to whom you are ministering.

A woman who came to me for counseling some time ago was in the midst of a difficult situation and was upset because a friend had suggested that she thank God for the problems she was experiencing.

"I can't believe she'd say that," the woman exclaimed. "That's ridiculous! It's insensitive! How can I thank God for being hurt?" She continued to vent her frustration.

After a while I asked, "I wonder what she meant by her comment."

"What do you mean?" she replied.

"Well, did she mean to thank God for this specific crisis as though it were good in and of itself or to thank God for using this situation so that you can change and grow. Could that be it?"

"Well . . . I don't know," she ventured.

"I know it hurts and your family wishes it had never occurred," I said, "But it did. So the past can't be changed and you feel out of control. Perhaps you can't change what happens in the future, but you can control your response to whatever occurs. It's just something to think about."

She did think about it and *in time* she came to the place of thanking God for being with her and allowing her this time of growth.

"One day I thought about the choices I had," she said. "I could depend on God, thank him and praise him and allow him to work through me. This didn't seem so bad when I considered the alternative!"

What kind of growth can we expect for the counselee? And what about our own growth? Lloyd Ogilvie suggests some of the things we can learn as we go through the difficult valleys in life.

First, it has been in the valleys of waiting for answers to my prayers that I have made the greatest strides in growing in the Lord's grace.

Second, it's usually in retrospect, after the strenuous period is over, that I can look back with gratitude for what I've received of the Lord Himself. I wouldn't trade the deeper trust and confidence I experienced from the valley for a smooth and trouble-free life.

Third, I long to be able to remember what the tough

times provide in my relationship with the Lord, so that when new valleys occur, my first reaction will be to thank and praise the Lord in advance for what is going to happen in and through me as a result of what happens to me. I really want my first thought to be, "Lord, I know You didn't send this, but You have allowed it and will use it as a part of working all things together for good. I trust you completely, Lord!" [8]

This attitude doesn't negate the turmoil of a difficult, ongoing problem or sudden crisis. People in crisis feel like the disciples adrift in that small boat during the storm on the Sea of Galilee. The waves throw them about and just as they get their legs under them, they're hit from another direction. The disciples struggled on the Sea of Galilee and all of us struggle on the sea of life. Each of us is afraid of capsizing. All we see are the waves which seem to grow each moment. Fear prevails. Our counselees need to hear the words of Jesus, "It is I, do not be afraid" (John 6:20).

We too often ask God, "Where are you?" as we pray for change and healing and stability in the life of the counselee. But *he is there* in the midst of the problem. We all ask him, "When? When will you answer?" As the psalmist cried, "How long, O Lord? Wilt thou forget me for ever? How long wilt thou hide thy face from me? How long must I bear pain in my soul, and have sorrow in my heart all the day? How long shall my enemy be exalted over me?" (Ps. 13:1, 2) That person in your office wants God to act according to his or her timetable, but the Scripture says, "Be still before the Lord, and wait patiently for him . . ." (Psalm 37:7). We become restless in waiting. And to block out the pain of waiting, we may be driven into frantic activity. This does not help, however, but resting before the Lord does.

Often waiting is a time of darkening clouds. Our skies do not lighten. Instead, everything seems to become even more grim.

Yet the darkening of our skies may forecast the dawn. It is in the gathering folds of deepening shadows that

God's hidden work for us takes place. The present, no matter how painful, is of utmost importance.

Somewhere, where our eyes cannot see and our ears are unable to hear, God is. And God is at work.[9]

In anger your counselee may tell you that she feels God is not doing anything! Why? Because she wants results *now*. The instant solution philosophy of our society often invades our perspective of God. People complain about waiting for a few weeks or days, but to God a day is as a thousand years and a thousand years an instant. God works in hidden ways even when you and your counselee are totally frustrated by no response. We are just unaware that he is active. Hear the words of Isaiah for the people then, and for us now:

Since ancient times no one has heard,
  no ear has perceived,
no eye has seen any God besides you,
  who acts on behalf of those who wait for him.
You come to the help of those who gladly do right,
  who remember your ways. (Isa. 64:4–5).

God has a reason for everything he does and a timetable for when he does it. " 'For I know the plans I have for you,' says the Lord, 'plans for welfare and not for evil, to give you a future and a hope' " (Jer. 29:11). Encourage your counselees to give themselves permission not to know what, not to know how, and not to know when. Even though they feel adrift on the turbulent ocean, God is holding them and knows the direction of their drift. Giving themselves permission to wait can give them hope. It is all right for God to ask any of us to wait for weeks and months and even years. During that time when we do not receive the answer and/or solution we think we need, he gives us his presence. "But I trust in thee, O, Lord; I say, 'Thou art my God. My times are in thy hands' " (Ps. 31:14, 15).

A passage of scripture that I have been learning to apply

for almost twenty years is one which I often share with those in counseling. It is found in James 1:2, 3: "Count it all joy, my brethren, when you meet various trials, for you know that the testing [or trying] of your faith produces steadfastness." It's easy to read a passage like this and say, "Well, that's fine." It is another thing, however, to put it into practice and actually experience it.

What does the word *consider* actually mean? It refers to an internal attitude of the heart or the mind that allows a trial and circumstance of life to affect one either adversely or beneficially. Another way James 1:2 might be translated is: "Make up your mind to regard adversity as something to welcome or be glad about."

Each of us has the power to decide what our attitude will be. We can approach the problem and say: "That's terrible. Totally upsetting. That is the last thing I wanted for my life. Why did it have to happen now? Why me?"

The other way of "considering" the same difficulty is to say: "It's not what I wanted or expected, but it's here. There are going to be some difficult times, but how can I make the best of them?" This does not mean denying the pain or the hurt that you might have to go through, but always asking, "What can I learn from it? How can I grow through this? How can it be used for God's glory?"

The verb tense used in the word *consider* indicates a decisiveness of action. It's not an attitude of resignation—"Well, I'll just give up. I'm stuck with this problem. That's the way life is." If you resign yourself, you will sit back and not put forth any effort. The verb tense actually indicates that you will have to go against your natural inclination to see the trial as a negative force. There will be some moments when you won't see it like that at all, and then you'll have to remind yourself: "No, I think there is a better way of responding to this. Lord, I really want you to help me see it from a different perspective." Then your mind will shift to a more constructive response. This often takes a lot of work on the part of the person experiencing the difficulty and yet—what have we said throughout this book about the Holy Spirit's working in all of our attitudes and thoughts?

God created all of us with both the capacity and the freedom to determine how we will respond to those unexpected incidents life brings our way.

During the time of crisis as well as all the other times of life, our stability comes from our Lord. God's Word says:

"Now to him who is able to strengthen you according to my gospel and the preaching of Jesus Christ, according to the revelation of the mystery which was kept secret for long ages . . ." (Rom. 16:25).

"Then he said to them, 'Go your way, eat the fat and drink sweet wine and send portions to him for whom nothing is prepared; for this day is holy to our Lord; and do not be grieved, for the joy of the Lord is your strength' " (Neh. 8:10).

"And he will be the stability of your times, abundance of salvation, wisdom, and knowledge; the fear of the Lord is his treasure" (Isa. 33:6).

Sure it hurts, but what can you do? What a tragedy if there is no way out.

But there is a way out. This is the message of the Bible. *You can have courage for crisis living!* You can take it! Crisis is the overture. Hurt is the introduction. Courage is the climax. And God is the ultimate resource.

This is the message of Job: "Though he [God] slay me, yet will I trust in him . . ." (Job 13:15 KJV). This is the message of David: "Yea, though I walk through the valley of the shadow of death, I will fear no evil; for thou art with me; thy rod and thy staff they comfort me" (Ps. 23:4 KJV). This is the message of Isaiah: "Thou wilt keep him in perfect peace, whose mind is stayed on thee, because he trusteth in thee" (Is. 26:3 KJV). This is the message of Paul: "For I am persuaded, that neither death, nor life, nor angels, nor principalities, nor powers, nor things present, nor things to come, nor height, nor depth, nor any other creature, shall be able to separate us from the love of God, which is in Christ Jesus our Lord" (Rom. 8:38, 39 KJV).

Considering it all joy leads us both to recognize and rejoice in him. We are, therefore, first of all to praise God for who he is as a response to his love, his goodness, his faithfulness, and his unbelievable concern for each one of us. If we learn to praise God, in difficult times we can recognize his sovereignty and his capacity. In praising God we are making a transfer—giving trust and dependence to him, rather than trusting and depending upon our own efforts and abilities.

Can you imagine someone sending you a letter admonishing you twenty times to rejoice—and four of those times to rejoice always? Ask your counselees that same question. Yet this is the type of letter Paul wrote to the church at Thessalonica. When any of us rejoice in the Lord, it is not because we feel like it. It is an act of our will, a commitment. When we rejoice in the Lord, we begin to see life from another point of view. Praise is the means of gaining a new perspective and new guidance for our bogged down lives.

Praising God in advance of a solution is an act of faith, a way of saying, "I don't know the outcome, but I am willing to trust." Sometimes I take a book and hand it to my client and ask the person to read a particular paragraph aloud. Then we talk about it. This quote is one of the paragraphs I use.

> Praising the Lord makes us willing and releases our imaginations to be used by Him to form the picture of what He is seeking to accomplish. A resistant will makes us very uncreative and lacking in adventuresome vision in the use of our capacity of imagination. God wants to use our imagination in the painting of the picture of what He is leading us to dare to hope for and expect. We become what we envision under *the Spirit's guidance.* That's why our own image of ourselves, other people, our goals, and our projects all need the inspiration of our imagination. However, until the Holy Spirit begins His work releasing it, our will keeps our imagination stunted and immature.[10]

Praise makes a difference because it is an act of relinquishment. It allows God to help us get ready for the next step, I am not just talking about crisis praying, but the development of a consistent pattern of praise. Praising means that we thank him for the fact that the answer is coming, and we will wait for it. We need God's perspective of our lives and the solutions we are seeking. Praise is the healer of life's pains, and change is possible especially for those of us who are new creations in Christ.

The excitement of ministering to people in the counseling office exists because of the potential of changed lives. And lives can change when prayer is part of the process of counseling. This perspective can come through praise.

CHAPTER EIGHT

PRACTICAL APPLICATIONS

AS A MINISTER OR PROFESSIONAL COUNSELOR you will be working with many individuals who struggle with worry, anxiety, depression, disappointment, impulsiveness, anger, and rage. In this chapter I would like to show how the approach suggested in the earlier chapters can help resolve some of these difficulties.

DEPRESSION

In offering help to the depressed individual, it is important to remember the following facts about depression:

1. There are numerous causes for depression, such as loss, repressed anger, negative thinking, low self-esteem, poor eat-

ing and sleeping habits, and other physical problems.

2. Depression is not a sin nor is a Christian sinning by being depressed.

3. Depression is a symptom or a warning system telling us that there is some specific cause which we need to discover.

4. Not attending to the first indications of depression is dangerous; if we ignore its warning it will intensify.

It is important to become knowledgeable about this common malady which you have probably experienced yourself at one time or another.[1]

One of the most effective ways to help a depressed individual, after you have ruled out a physical cause, is to use the cognitive and behavioral approach. We need to tailor our approach to the uniqueness of the person's depression and to his or her personality. A highly-structured problem-solving approach is one of the best techniques.

When an individual becomes depressed, his thinking process changes. He begins to misinterpret his experiences and his perspective about himself. Some individuals create their state of depression because of this bent toward negative thinking.

As a person enters into the state of depression, he tends to regard himself, his life, his experiences, and his future in a negative way. Many depressed individuals feel they have lost something or failed in some way and, therefore, they are doomed for the rest of their lives. This is not a rational belief but one based upon the emotion of the depression. Any activity undertaken will have a negative outcome and the negative thinking begins to move in a vicious cycle, gaining intensity and momentum with every circle completed.

To understand the thinking process of a depressed person, look at three faulty thought patterns that distort the individual's total view of life. These can be called the Depressive Triad.

The first part of the Depressive Triad is concerned with a person looking at his experiences in a negative manner. This gives him a negative view of the world. He interprets (rightly or wrongly) his interactions with the world as representing defeat, disparagement, or deprivation. All of life is filled with burdens and obstacles, and this *negative thinking can lead to depression. When one is depressed he or she continues to*

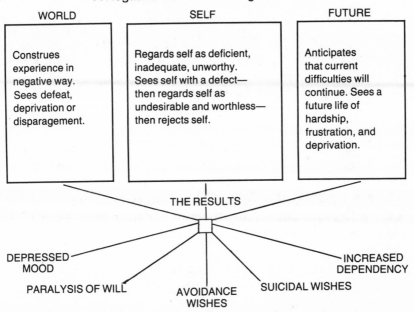

DEPRESSIVE TRIAD[2]
A Negative View of Thinking Patterns

WORLD	SELF	FUTURE
Construes experience in negative way. Sees defeat, deprivation or disparagement.	Regards self as deficient, inadequate, unworthy. Sees self with a defect— then regards self as undesirable and worthless— then rejects self.	Anticipates that current difficulties will continue. Sees a future life of hardship, frustration, and deprivation.

THE RESULTS

DEPRESSED MOOD   PARALYSIS OF WILL   AVOIDANCE WISHES   SUICIDAL WISHES   INCREASED DEPENDENCY

think more and more negatively, which reinforces the depression.

The person with a negative view of the world interprets his experiences as actually detracting from himself. Even neutral experiences are interpreted in a negative manner. A neutral attitude on the part of a friend is seen as rejection. A neutral comment is interpreted as a hostile remark. His thinking pattern is clouded by reading into the remarks of other people whatever fits his previously drawn negative conclusions.

A young man had a straight A average in college the first three years. But whenever other students were asked for their comments in class he would think, *Why didn't the professor call on me? He must think I'm dumb. Maybe I am. Anyone can get A's. That doesn't mean anything.* A person views himself in an impossible manner, which doesn't leave any way out. Another young college student rarely spoke up in class and thought, *I bet they think I'm stupid because I don't say*

157

anything. When he did speak he thought, *They must think I talk too much.* No matter what he did he saw himself with a defect and ended up rejecting himself.

The last pattern evident in the depressive pattern is the negative view of the future. "No hope" is the cry! *If I'm a failure now, I will always be a failure. If people don't like me now, that will never change. The current situation has no time limit and will continue!*

In pondering the future, the individual makes assumptions and selective abstractions, generalizing and magnifying events and remarks way out of proportion. He is so predisposed to negative thinking that he automatically makes negative interpretations of situations. Defeat is his watchword.

Our self-talk is the culprit that fosters negative thinking leading to depression. Our thoughts create many of our feelings. Note the following sequence in the growth of feelings and behavior.

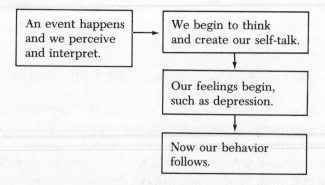

As you listen to your counselees you will hear what has just been described many times. It may be helpful to separate what you have heard into individual components. You could actually start with any of the symptoms that you have heard, such as, the emotional, the motivational, the thought processes, the behavioral or even physiological, and work toward changing the symptom cluster they have told you. By doing this, you will find it easier to work with the individual and he or she will begin to feel that something tangible is happening in life.

As you assist the depressed individual, it is important to

teach him or her how to define his or her situation specifically and to include the details. This includes the external events that are occurring as well as the person's inner conversations. Here is a portion of a counseling interview:

Counselee: Well, I've been depressed and, uh . . . upset lately.

Minister: How long has this been occurring?

Counselee: About a month, I guess. Yes, about a month. I think a lot of it stems from the fact that my husband has started working late with overtime. We need the money, so that's good. I guess I should be more grateful.

Minister: In what way is your depression and feeling upset tied into your husband working late?

Counselee: (pause) Well, I feel lonely in the evening waiting for him. And I also feel upset and nervous. I don't like being alone in the evening or late at night. And he's so tired when he gets home that we don't have any time together. He just falls into bed exhausted.

Minister: So even when he comes home, you end up being somewhat alone. You don't have much time with him at all.

Counselee: That's right. (She showed a bit more feeling as she talked now.) I miss our times of talking together about the day. And it's not just me feeling like that. He misses it too. And we're both unhappy about our lack of sex.

Minister: What do you feel this is due to . . . the lack of sex?

Counselee: Exhaustion! Nothing else. Before this, sex was great. He's just too tired.

Minister: One of your main concerns then is the lack of contact with your husband. It's lacking in conversation, sexual and. . . .

Counselee: Yes, and I don't like being alone at night. I would rather be with another person. I do have a number of friends and enjoy them too. I just feel stuck with no options.

Minister: So it's a combination of missing your husband and also being alone as well.

Counselee: Yes . . . (pause). Well, there is something else that bothers me. I am frightened to be alone at night. We live on a dark street with few lights. I think about the possibility of someone discovering that I'm at home alone and breaking in. I jump whenever I hear a noise and my mind starts going wild. If I try to go to sleep before John gets home, I can't. And then I'm tired each day from the late hours.

Minister: Before your husband began to work overtime, was any of this a problem?

Counselee: Not really. . . . I think most of it is because of this situation.

Minister: How much do you think about your situation each day?

Counselee: Most of the time. I think about how I don't like it and I worry about what might happen. I just don't know what to do about it.

Minister: Can you tell me some of the actual thoughts you have about your situation? Give me some examples.

The session continued with several examples and the minister then proceeded to assist this wife in discovering the connection between her situation, her thoughts, and depression. As they worked together for several additional sessions, the inner conversations began to take a different direction and several practical options were explored, such as finding a babysitter in order to go out and see friends occasionally, getting better locks for the door as well as a watch dog, and finding other times for sex with her husband.

Even if your goal is to alter the thinking process of the person, you don't always tackle the thinking process head-on initially. Perhaps the symptoms of the person sitting in your office are sadness, apathy, crying, lack of caring, a depressed posture, etc. You could approach such an individual by helping to change his behavior and mobilize him to take some action. This would help him feel better about himself, as though there were some hope, and he would actually see some change. You would be helping him provide himself with the fuel he needs to change his thought processes. This is a key factor, for with some individuals you need to begin with behavior. Your goal is to change his thought life, but changing his behavior is a step toward that goal. Engaging in positive activities can counter the misbelief that says, *The future is totally hopeless. I can't do anything. All of life is unpleasant.*

Having the person visualize positive scenes or a psalm as you read it to him challenges the belief that "all life is unpleasant." What you are doing is using several different approaches to help him change his thinking.

FIVE BEHAVIOR APPROACHES FOR DEALING WITH DEPRESSION

Here are five behavior approaches suggested by Aaron Beck that can be very effective.

1. *Success Therapy or Graded Task Assignment.* The purpose of this approach is to give the person some task to accomplish in which he can be successful. A simple assignment is given at first which is within the person's capability. One person might be given the assignment of boiling an egg for breakfast and working up gradually to an entire meal for himself, and then for the family. Each time the person completes an assignment, a sense of success and accomplishment counters his feelings of depression.

2. *Mastery and Pleasure Therapy* (or M & P Therapy). The depressed person is asked to keep a list of his activities and mark down an "M" for each mastery experience and a "P" for each pleasure experience. A depressed person is blind to the fact that he can accomplish some things and is also blind to satisfaction he receives. His recall is limited. Even though he may have experienced something worthwhile or achieved a task, he does not remember it and says, "I can't do anything anymore." By recognizing, labeling, writing down, and recalling mastery experiences, a person is able to see that he is capable and he can achieve satisfaction. He discovers that he has many more pleasure experiences than he thought.

You may help the person list some activities that he was able to accomplish prior to being depressed to show that he has been capable. The same can be done for pleasurable activities. Sometimes a person is asked to keep a running account of his activities hour by hour so he can see the pleasurable or successful events in greater detail.

3. *Activity Scheduling.* Another method that has been used successfully is to schedule activities with the person. Since this person probably sees himself as ineffective, he needs to

be active in order to see himself as potentially more effective. A schedule helps him to structure his day. But remember, depressed persons tend to resist attempts to get them to be "busy." You can suggest that being busy will perhaps relieve some of his unpleasant feelings to a degree.

4. *Alternative Therapy.* This method contains two different parts. One is to consider alternative explanations for his experiences, which may help him see the bias in his interpretations. The other is to consider alternative ways of dealing with his problems. By his doing this, problems that he thought were unsolvable may not seem so impossible to him after all.

5. *Cognitive Rehearsal.* In this technique the counselor helps the person deal with what he feels are the problems keeping him from carrying out his plans or achieving his goals. He is asked to imagine himself going through the steps necessary to reach his goal and report the various obstacles he expects and the conflicts these bring about. All of these conflicts and obstacles can be discussed and actually overcome through the discussion which frees up the person to begin to work again.[3]

What are the results of using these approaches with the depressed person? The person's self-concept can be changed as he now sees himself as being more masterful and he also becomes more optimistic. He is distracted from his painful depressive thoughts and feelings because of his new work and activity. Other people's responses become more positive and he sees them as being more positive. He begins to enjoy what he is doing and thus can feel better.

Here is an example of how these can be put to use in a person's life. A depressed person has come to see you and states that his problems are those of withdrawal and avoiding people. He has begun a lifestyle of inactivity. Now he begins to give some reasons for not trying. He may say that he is too tired or weak to try and it is really pointless to try to change. He also feels that he will feel worse if he is active and he will fail at anything he tries.

If you were helping this person, you could ask some questions such as, "What do you have to lose by trying? Has being inactive done you any good? Most people do feel worse if

they are passive. How do you know that you will fail at anything that you try?" These questions thoughtfully posed and
discussed may penetrate his defenses against trying. You could
then work out with this person some of the techniques such
as activity schedules, graded task assignments, and cognitive
rehearsals.

Not every individual will go along with your suggestions
for changing his or her behavior, so let me suggest a step-
by-step approach before we look at some of the specifics of
the thought-changing process.

Step 1—Suggest a specific project for the person you are
counseling to accomplish.

Step 2—Draw out his or her reasons or objections to what
you have suggested.

Step 3—Ask the person to evaluate the validity of his or
her objections.

Step 4—Share with the person why these reasons or beliefs
are invalid and how they are self-defeating.

Step 5—Challenge the counselee's interest in trying to accomplish the suggested assignment.

Step 6—Set up the project in such a manner that he will
be able to accomplish it (break it into small steps) and that
he will be able to measure his accomplishment. By completing
the task, he counters his false belief that he cannot accomplish
anything.

Step 7—After the counselee has had this successful experience, share with the person how this success contradicts his
self-defeating predictions. The best way of doing this is to
draw it from him through your questions.

Step 8—Review with the person the new "positive" and
"objective" attitudes proposed by you. Use imagery exercises
and prayer with him at this point.

Step 9—Train him to identify his negative thoughts, challenge them and develop reasonable answers to them. This
is where the homework comes into your counseling approach.[4]

Here is a simple way to proceed.

The first step is to identify the self-talk and the events that
help to create its occurrence. Many of my depressed clients

use a journal in which they record at least one event each day. The figure below is an example.

I ask my counselees to identify the event (Column A) and record the accompanying emotion or feeling in Column C. Then, as accurately as they can recall, they are to describe their self-talk in Column B, to remember the things they said to themselves at that time. Often thoughts and beliefs go unnoticed. The more hidden and automatic the thoughts are, the greater power and influence they have over us. Bringing them into the light of awareness diminishes their power.

When the self-talk has been identified the next step is for the person to counter it, argue with it, or dispute it. Questions such as the following should be asked as they complete Column D:

1. Is it possible to rationally support this belief?
2. What evidence is there that this is true?
3. What is the worst possible thing that could occur even if this is true?
4. Is there any reason why I should or must? Whenever you say "should," be sure to ask the question, "Why should I?"

Date	A. Event	B. Self-Talk	C. Feeling	D. Dispute
9/20	Lost my temper with the kids.	"I shouldn't ever yell at the children. I'm a terrible mother."	Depression	
9/21	Forgot an appointment with a friend.	"Jim must really be annoyed with me. I'm sure he thinks I'm mad at him and thinks I intentionally stood him up."	Worried and guilty.	
9/22	Attempted to pray.	"God is angry with me or he wouldn't be leaving me feeling so abandoned and unconsoled. This is a sure sign that I'm unforgivably bad; even God has given up on me." [5]	Emptiness, doubt, and guilt.	

Sometimes the questions you ask can help the counselees see how hard they are on themselves with their negative self statements.

You might ask, "Suppose I made mistakes the way you say that you do? Would you despise and loathe me for it?" This may help them to see how exaggerated their own responses are toward themselves. "How do you think I would be able to do my job if someone were standing behind me looking over my shoulder and criticizing what I did? This is what you are doing to yourself." I wonder what you could say to yourself that would be more realistic and helpful to you?

PERFECTIONISM

One of the contributing factors to depression, frustration, and anger is the perfectionistic attitude or belief syndrome. Let's consider this in light of false beliefs.

The best time to work on perfectionistic tendencies is not when a person is depressed but at a time when he can be objective about himself. Your goal is to help him break loose from perfectionism. Ask:

"What is your motivation for being a perfectionist?"

Have the person make a list of the advantages and disadvantages of perfectionism. He may discover that the disadvantages actually outweigh the advantages. He may discover that he *is* able to accomplish tasks, but in so doing he becomes tense, irritable, fearful of trying anything new, intolerant of others who do things differently, and depressed when failure occurs.

One of the beliefs that the counselee may have is that unless a person aims for perfection he can never be happy; life can't be enjoyed or offer any satisfaction unless he attains this goal. This belief can be tested with your counselee by using an antiperfectionism form. Have the person record on the form the actual amount of satisfaction he gets from his activities. These could include eating a steak, mowing the lawn, fixing a broken toaster, preparing a talk, washing the car, etc. Then have him estimate how *perfectly* he did each task (using a scale of 0–100) as well as how *satisfying* each task was (using the same scale).

The purpose of this activity is to show him that his satisfaction is not dependent upon being perfect. Here is an example of a physician who believed that he had to be perfect.

Activity	Record How Effectively You Did This Between 0 and 100%	Record How Satisfying This Was Between 0 and 100%
Fix the broken pipe in kitchen.	20% (I took a long time and made a lot of mistakes.)	99% (I actually did it!)
Give lecture to medical school class.	98% (I got a standing ovation.)	50% (I usually get a standing ovation—I wasn't particularly thrilled with my performance.)
Play tennis after work.	60% (I lost the match but played okay.)	95% (Really felt good. Enjoyed the game and the exercise.)
Edit draft of my latest paper for one hour.	75% (I stuck with it and corrected many errors, and smoothed out the sentences.)	15% (I kept telling myself it wasn't the definitive paper and felt quite frustrated.)
Talk to student about his career options.	50% (I didn't do anything special. I just listened to his obvious suggestions.)	90% (He really seemed to appreciate our talk, so I felt turned on.)

Fear is often a motivating factor in perfectionism. I remember a college student I worked with many years ago who was almost a compulsive perfectionist. He came from a home where you earned love by performing. If you attempted something and failed, then no love was forthcoming. Because of this he ran into difficulties. His fear of failing was also enhanced by obsessive thoughts that interrupted his ability to concentrate. School failure was the worst for him. Thus at college he dropped out of school the first four semesters at final exam time because he did not want to attempt the exams and fail. (Failure in his eyes was anything less than a strong A.)

For years he crippled himself with his perfectionism. Fortunately, he received the help he needed through counseling. After he was married and working, he went back to college part-time, willing to do his best and accept whatever he could accomplish. His first twelve courses produced A's for him!

Fears often enter our mind automatically. They are part of our deeper, hidden self-talk that emerges from time to time as a means of hindering us. Here is the example of a college student who was afraid of submitting a term paper because it had to be "just right." The student was told to list his automatic thoughts and then identify the fear by using the vertical-arrow method. This approach is similar to peeling off the outside layers of an onion until the origins of the perfectionism are discovered. This process can be very enlightening as deeper fears that have been covered over are discovered. Here is Jeffrey's journey.

Automatic Thoughts	Rational Responses
1. I didn't do an excellent job on the paper. "If that were true, why would it be a problem?"	1. All-or-nothing thinking. The paper is pretty good, even though it's not perfect.
2. The professor will notice all the typos and the weak sections. "And why would that be a problem?"	2. Mental filter. He probably will notice typos, but he'll read the whole paper. There are some fairly good sections.
3. He'll feel that I didn't care about it. "Suppose he does. What then?"	3. Mind reading. I don't know that he will think this. If he did, it wouldn't be the end of the world. A lot of students don't care about their papers. Besides, I do care about it, so if he thought this he'd be wrong.
4. I'll be letting him down. "If that were true and he did feel that way, why would it be upsetting to me?"	4. All-or-nothing thinking; fortune teller error. I can't please everyone all the time. He's liked most of my work. If he does feel disappointed in this paper he can survive.

Automatic Thoughts	Rational Responses
5. I'll get a D or an F on the paper. "Suppose I did—what then?"	5. Emotional reasoning; fortune teller error. I feel this way because I'm upset. But I can't predict the future. I might get a B or a C, but a D or an F isn't very likely.
6. That would ruin my academic record. "And then what would happen?"	6. All-or-nothing thinking; fortune teller error. Other people goof up at times, and it doesn't seem to ruin their lives. Why can't I goof up at times?
7. That would mean I wasn't the kind of student I was supposed to be. "Why would that be upsetting to me?"	7. "Should" statement. Who laid down the rule that I was "supposed" to be a certain way at all times? Who said I was predestined and morally obliged to live up to some particular standard?
8. People will be angry with me. I'll be a failure. "And suppose they were angry and I was a failure? Why would that be so terrible?"	8. The fortune teller error. If someone is angry with me, it's his/her problem. I can't be pleasing people all the time—it's too exhausting. It makes my life a tense, constricted, rigid mess. Maybe I'd do better to set my own standards and risk someone's anger. If I fail at the paper, it certainly doesn't make me a failure.
9. Then I would be ostracized and alone. "And then what?"	9. The fortune teller error. Everyone won't ostracize me!
10. If I'm alone, I'm bound to be miserable.	10. Disqualifying positive data. Some of my happiest times have been when I'm alone. My "misery" has nothing to do with being alone, but comes from the fear of disapproval and from persecuting myself for not living up to perfectionistic standards.[6]

168

It is helpful to suggest that each answer or counter be reinforced with imagery and prayer. An answer may lend itself to being visualized in detail in order to strengthen its usage. Each answer or counter can be shared aloud in prayer. Requests for further clarification of answers and thankfulness for what insights have occurred can also be part of the prayer.

ANGER

Numerous individuals struggle throughout life with anger and rage. They, too, are people who can be helped, especially if they discover how their own self-talk or inner conversations create this emotion. It is important to be able to lead them step by step in the change process.

Anger can be either aggressive or assertive. Les Carter makes an interesting distinction between aggressive and assertive anger. Aggressive anger he defines as the emotion exhibited by persons who make a firm stand for their own convictions without demonstrating a concern for the needs of others. Assertive anger, on the other hand, is the emotion exhibited by those who take a firm stand for their own convictions while at the same time being considerate of the needs of all involved.[7]

Some counselees will express their aggressive anger by being loud and boisterous. Their feelings are expressed at a high decibel level. When frustration is intense, some people feel that shouting is the only way to make their point. Still others get their body into action by flapping their arms, gesturing with a fist, kicking, or stomping their feet. It is quite easy for this anger to cross the line into violence. Hitting the wall, the door, or another person is the final result of this emotional outburst.

Recently, a client and his wife came into my office for their weekly visit. Something was new—the man wore a cast on his right hand. I thought of joking with him and saying, "How did you break your hand? Hitting the wall?" But fortunately I did not. We proceeded through the session, and just before we closed I asked, "What happened?"

"Well," he said, "with all the upset and financial frustrations and the hassle around home the other night, I was so angry and frustrated that I slugged the wall. Unfortunately, the wall didn't give, and I knew right away by the pain that I broke a bone. I guess I learned that hitting something is not the best way to deal with my anger."

When people feed their anger in this way, unless they hit a wall and break a bone, there is a tendency for the anger to keep building. Self-control has flown away like a bird in flight, and reasoning with such a person at that time is futile.

Another demonstration of aggressive anger, which you will confront, is caustic, critical comments that put others down. Blame is often used, as is sarcasm. The person really does not have a desire to resolve the issues. The anger has a bite and a sting to it, and it is meant to be felt by the receiver.

Such anger leaves the recipient feeling totally frustrated, irritated, and disarmed. This approach does not resolve the problem, but is an invitation for continued warfare. Choosing to avoid open conflict causes bad feelings to fester and grow. You will see this in your marital and family counseling.

As you discuss anger, help your counselee understand that anger is a response or a symptom. Most anger comes from fear, hurt, or frustration and within these three self-talk can usually be found as the culprit. It is important that the counselee discover the cause.

One of the most basic principles to teach counselees concerned with their anger is to try to cut off their anger at the earliest possible moment. Their trigger point is the best place. There are actually four different stages at which they can deal with their anger. You may want to list these on a large chart to visually illustrate as you discuss them.

1. *You can deal with your anger when you are calm.* This is the best possible time to prepare yourself so you don't experience anger unnecessarily. Ask yourself:

"Do I make unnecessary demands upon myself? Upon others?"

"Do I set up realistic demands for myself? For others?"

If a person can begin to accept as a fact of life that people are imperfect, anger will lessen.

Suggest that the person write out how he or she would like to respond when irritations and annoyances occur. Ask the person to take the time to practice this new approach in his or her mind.

Here is an example of such an exercise. You may want to print this as a worksheet to give your counselee. Take the time to read through this material with your counselee in session and discuss the various points. By doing this, you may achieve greater follow-through and application.

If there is a situation or person who is constantly proving to be a source of irritation, picture yourself taking the action necessary to deal with the problem. Spend time imagining yourself responding to an irritating encounter in a nonirritating manner. Talk to the person involved and see if the two of you can remove the source of irritation. You may find it helpful to plot on the following chart the anger you usually feel.

Date   Time   Intensity of Anger   What I Became Angry At

                      Light   High

                      1   2   3   4   5

How I Respond   How I Want to Respond

If you can see a pattern to your anger what could you do to break that pattern?

2. The second possibility is to *cut off the anger before it begins.* No one is 100 percent consistent; there will be times when anger breaks through. But planning for a new response when you are not angry can help. It is possible to cut off your anger by becoming aware of the possible onset of anger. Two ways of doing this are identifying what other people do or say that makes you angry, and identifying the self-talk you use to create anger. Then write out substitute statements that will stop your self-talk from producing anger.

Statement	Counter
_____	_____
_____	_____
_____	_____
_____	_____
_____	_____
_____	_____
_____	_____
_____	_____
_____	_____

3. A third stage at which you can deal with anger is *when you are actually angry.* First, recognize and accept your anger. To resolve it, you need to admit and recognize it. Often we hear angry people shout, "I am *not* angry!" It may help to accept another person's evaluation of what is taking place. Assume that you are angry.

The next step is to give up your desire to strike back. If you are angered because you have been hurt, you will usually want to hurt back. In fact, not only do we want to hurt in return; we want to punish and make the person pay for what we think he has done. Romans 12:17–19 states, "Repay no one evil for evil, but take thought for what is noble in the sight of all. If possible, so far as it depends upon you, live peaceably with all. Beloved, never avenge yourselves, but leave it to the wrath of God. . . ." If we carry our anger it becomes resentment.

As you counsel, you may want to share some of the following information and situations with your counselee verbally.

One of my clients had a tendency to erupt over even the smallest irritation and disruption by his employees. Since he owned the business, there was little the workers could do. He was aware of his explosive nature and wanted to learn to respond differently. He also liked to be in control of his life and everything around him. When I said, "How does it feel to allow other people and situations to control you?" he was a bit taken aback.

He replied, "What do you mean, control me! I'm in control of my life."

"Well," I said, "on the one hand, you've said these other people, situations, and interruptions make you angry. If they do, don't they control you? If, on the other hand, you are in control of your life, you could choose not to respond in this angry manner."

He was stunned and silent. Eventually he admitted that he was in charge of his emotional responses. We then proceeded to work out a system of both delaying and short-circuiting his anger response and also a system for warning others that he might be in a bad mood. He went out and purchased small flags and placed them on his desk. Whenever he was in a good mood or handling responses fairly well, the green flag would be flying. If he started to become upset or at the first angry response, the green flag would be lowered and replaced by the yellow caution flag. Then when he was really angry and upset, the red flag would be raised. I was amazed at the effect of this visual reminder.

After one month the green flag had not been lowered once. My client said, "It's amazing how much the flag reminds me that I don't have to become upset and angry. This is something that can be controlled. And my staff appreciates both the warning system and the effect it's had on me already."

4. *Conscious delay* is a procedure that can be used to hold back angry or negative responses which have been generated in the mind. It is possible to edit negative thoughts (which is not the same as denying or repressing them) so that you will express yourself or behave in a positive manner. It is not hypocritical or dishonest to edit your thoughts. Ephesians 4:15 states that we are to speak the truth in love. A literal translation of this verse means that we are to speak the truth in such a way that our relationship is cemented together better than before. Totally blunt, let-it-all-hang-out honesty does not build relationships. By editing, you are aware of your thoughts and feelings and you are also controlling them. You are actually taking the energy produced by the anger and converting it into something useful that will build the relationship.

How is it possible to edit your thoughts when you begin to become angry? First of all, suggest that your counselee make a list of some of the behaviors of his or her spouse (or another person) to whom he or she responds with anger. Here are some examples:

- My spouse is usually late, as much as fifteen or twenty minutes. Whenever this happens I become angry.
- My spouse frequently overspends the monthly household allotment and doesn't tell me about it.
- My spouse leaves clothes and dishes around the house consistently and expects others to pick them up.
- Often when I set up an outing or a date for us (even well in advance) my spouse has already planned something for that time and hasn't told me in advance.

Now list the statements you make to yourself about each of these. What are some of the possible explanations for the way the other person is behaving? What are three alternate statements you could make to your spouse to replace your usual response? [8]

Statements
1.
2.
3.
4.

Possible Explanation
1.
2.
3.
4.

Alternate Statement
1.
2.
3.

All of us, at one time or another, use a variety of self-talk statements that tend to generate anger. David Burns describes some of these in his book *Feeling Good: The New Mood Therapy.* We have discussed these earlier, but it will be helpful to consider how you can share these with your counselees and assist them to evaluate their own thinking right in the sessions with you.[9]

On numerous occasions anger is caused by distorted thinking. As a person learns to replace distorted thoughts with realistic ones, irritability lessens and self-control increases. Here are some of the distortions that occur most frequently when anger exists.

One main offender is *labeling.* When someone describes a person whom he is mad at as "a klutz" or "stupid," that person is labeled and the impression is given that he or she is a bad individual. If a person is written off in this way, you catalog in your mind everything you don't like about him or her (which is mental filter) and discount or ignore his or her good points (disqualifying the positive). In doing this you create a false target for your anger.

Labeling is a distorted thinking process and it causes a person to feel morally superior or inappropriately indignant, or both. It is a way of building one's own self-image at the expense of someone else. Labeling makes it easy for us to blame another person toward whom we feel a need to retaliate. Labeling can also become a self-fulfilling prophecy.

After you have shared the above thoughts with the counselee, spend time helping him identify the labels he is using.

Mind reading is another type of thinking that generates anger. Motives are inventions that explain to our own satisfaction why another person did what he or she did. But we are dealing with a false premise. Our hypotheses do not describe the actual thoughts that motivated the other individual, and probably we have not taken the time to check out what we are saying to ourselves about the other person. In a given situation, ask your counselee what he or she assumed the other person was thinking or what his motives were.

Another form of anger-creating distortion is *magnification.* Whenever a negative event is exaggerated, the emotional reaction may be blown out of proportion. A man is driving on the freeway and the traffic comes to a halt. Five minutes later it is still at a standstill. The person begins saying to himself, *I can't take this! I can't stand this!* Is that true or is it an exaggeration? Isn't he taking it? Isn't he sitting there stuck in traffic experiencing what everyone else is experiencing? Since he is taking it, why tell himself he isn't? People do tolerate delays. He could give himself credit for sitting there. His only other alternative is to get out of his car and start walking, but not many people leave their cars sitting on the freeway while they walk away. Ask your counselee to think for a moment to see if he or she can remember any exaggerations he may have made.

One of the most important elements involved in reducing anger is to develop the desire to stop the anger. Once we are angry, it is difficult for us to stop the process of taking a verbal bite out of another person. The desire for revenge that frequently accompanies anger can be consuming. But there is a way to short-circuit this anger. Ask your counselee in session to make a list of the advantages and disadvantages of being angry and acting out revenge. Have him or her consider both the short-term and long-term consequences of anger. After the list is compiled, review it and ask, "Which are greater, the costs or the benefits of anger?" This usually helps the person realize there is a better way to respond than with anger and revenge. In addition to listing the advantages and disadvantages, ask him or her to go one step further and list the positive consequences that may result from not becoming angry.

David Burns, in *Feeling Good . . .* tells us how this process helped one of his clients named Sue. Sue had two daughters from a previous marriage while her husband, a hardworking lawyer, had a teenage daughter from his previous marriage. Since his time was limited, Sue tended to feel deprived, angry, and resentful. She was bitter because she felt her husband was not being fair to her in giving her enough time and attention. Sue then proceeded to list the advantages and disadvantages of her anger and concluded with a list of the possible positive consequences of not becoming angry. Here is the way her list looked.

Advantages of My Anger	Disadvantages of My Anger
1. It feels good.	1. I will be souring my relationship with John even more.
2. John will understand that I strongly disapprove of him.	2. He will want to reject me.
3. I have the *right* to blow my stack if I want to.	3. I will often feel guilty and down on myself after I blow my stack.
4. He'll know I'm not a doormat.	4. He will probably retaliate against me, since he doesn't like being taken advantage of either.
5. I'll show him I won't tolerate being taken advantage of.	5. My anger inhibits both of us from correcting the problem that caused the anger in the first place. It prevents resolution and sidetracks us from dealing with the issues.
6. Even though I don't get what I want, I can at least have the satisfaction of getting revenge. I can make him squirm and feel hurt like I do. Then he'll have to shape up.	6. One minute I'm up, one minute I'm down. My irritability makes John and the people around me never know what to expect. I get labeled as moody and cranky and spoiled and immature. They see me as a childish brat.
	7. I might make neurotics out of my kids. As they grow up, they may resent my explosions and see me as someone to stay away from rather than to go to for help.
	8. John may leave me if he gets enough of my nagging and complaining.
	9. The unpleasant feelings I create make me feel miserable. Life becomes a sour and bitter experience, and I miss out on the joy and creativity I used to prize so highly.[10]

The possible consequences of *not* becoming angry were:

Possible Consequences
1. People will like me better. They will want to be near me.
2. I will be more predictable.
3. I will be in better control of my emotions.
4. I will be more relaxed.
5. I will be more comfortable with myself.
6. I will be viewed as a positive, nonjudgmental, practical person.
7. I will behave more often as an adult than as a selfish child.
8. I will influence people more effectively.
9. My kids, husband, and parents will respect me more.

Suggest to the person you are counseling that he keep a journal and list irritating situations which seem to plague him. Ask him to take time each day to evaluate those situations, and then reread what he wrote. He may be surprised at the controlling effect of this procedure. He needs to continue to do this day after day.

The following outline has been helpful for those struggling with anger, worry, guilt, low self-esteem, and other difficulties. Have the outline duplicated and give a copy to your counselee to use during the week.

Monitor!

One way to improve the content of your self-talk is to monitor it. Here is a suggestion to help you become aware of your internal conversations.

1. Each hour, check your thoughts. Set an alarm on your watch or some other device to alert you every hour.

2. When you signal yourself, stop whatever you are doing and review the thoughts you have been experiencing. What was the conversation you were having with yourself? Write down your thoughts in a sentence. What statements were you making that contributed to your anger or to being upset? What were the sentences?

———————————————————————
———————————————————————
———————————————————————
———————————————————————
———————————————————————

3. Review each sentence by asking yourself these questions:

Question	Answer
• Is it true?	
• How do I know it is true?	
• Where is the evidence?	
• Am I overreacting?	
• Will this be true twelve hours from now?	
• What is another possible response?	
• What are the consequences of this path of thinking?	
• Now counter any negative self-talk with positive realistic statements.[11]	

Imagery Exercises

I find that imagery exercises work very well in the control and reduction of anger. These exercises can be started within the counseling session and continued at home.

Ask your counselee to indicate in order of importance the five most anger-creating situations he is currently experiencing. Then have him close his eyes and imagine becoming angry as he is accustomed to doing. Suggest that he hear the statements he usually says to himself, see himself responding in anger in the usual way, and feel the emotion of anger in his body.

Now have him take a minute to relax and imagine himself in the same situation, but this time making rational, calm statements. Ask him to see himself responding in the way he would like to respond . . . see himself putting into practice the scriptural guidelines of "being slow to anger" . . . feel himself responding in a relaxed and calm manner . . . hear himself making calm, balanced statements. He will be able to change his angry reactions if he will spend time in advance visualizing a response in the desired fashion.

Suggest that the counselee practice this new version of the experience in his mind again and again until he feels comfortable and competent. When he confronts the real situation, a new response is possible. Have him take each of the angry situations he has identified and go through the same process he just completed.

Counseling entails creativity, skill, mental alertness, and reliance upon the presence of the Holy Spirit. Many suggestions have been made so far and you will find yet others in the Appendix to follow.

Every suggested approach and technique will need to be adapted to the unique situation and problem presented to you by each counselee. Perhaps what has been shared in the book will give you direction, some structure, and the challenge to be cautiously creative. Think of yourself as an invited guest into the life of another person to help that person grow. To develop your skills, read through this book again, practice and refine your counseling skills by role playing cases with your colleagues, listen to your counseling tapes, and invite Jesus Christ to be present every minute of the counseling hours.

APPENDIX I

SUGGESTED METHODS FOR CONTROLLING THOUGHTS

Thought stopping is a very helpful procedure to assist with many of life's difficulties, such as fear, anxiety, depression, anger, and perfectionistic tendencies. In the late 1950s, many therapists used it in treating those with obsessive and phobic thoughts. Obsessions are repetitive and intrusive trains of thought that are unrealistic, unproductive, and, often, anxiety provoking.

An obsessive person is sometimes called an "overworrier." Obsessions may take the form of self-doubt: "I will never be able to do this job right" or, "I'm too plain to get a date." Obsessions may also take the form of fear: "I wonder if something is wrong with my heart" or, "If they raise the rent, I'll have to move."

Thought stopping involves concentrating on the unwanted thoughts and, after a short time, suddenly stopping and emptying one's mind. The command "Stop!" or a loud noise is generally used to interrupt the unpleasant thoughts. There are three explanations for the success of thought stopping:

1. The command "Stop!" serves as a punishment. Behavior that is consistently punished is likely to be inhibited.

2. The command "Stop!" acts as a distraction that is incompatible with obsessive or phobic thoughts.

3. Thought stopping is an assertive response and needs to be followed by positive thought substitutions, that is, reassuring or self-accepting statements. For example, a person says, "These big 747s are awfully safe" instead of, "Look at that wing shake, I bet it's ready to come off." This is where the use of positive passages from God's Word can be so helpful. Imagining the safe takeoff and landing with prayer is also involved in this process.

It has been well established that negative and frightening thoughts invariably create negative and frightening emotions. If thoughts can be controlled, the overall stress level can be significantly reduced. For this to be effective, thought stopping must be practiced conscientiously throughout the day for several weeks with consistency.

The first step is to explore and list the stressful thoughts. Then use the following stressful thoughts inventory [1] with your counselees to help them assess which recurrent thoughts are the most painful and intrusive.

Stressful Thoughts Inventory

On the questionnaire that begins on p. 183, put a check mark after each item that applies to you. For items you check, rate them in column A from 1 to 5, based on these statements:

1. *Sensible.* This is quite a sensible and reasonable thing for me to think.
2. *Habit.* This is just a habit. I think it automatically without really worrying about it.
3. *Not necessary.* I often realize that this thought is not really necessary, but I don't try to stop it.
4. *Try to stop.* I know this thought is not necessary. It bothers me, and I try to stop it.
5. *Try very hard to stop.* This thought upsets me a great deal, and I try very hard to stop it.

For items that you check, rate them in column B from 1 to 4, based on the following statements:

1. *No interference.* This thought does not interfere with other activities.
2. *Interferes a little.* This thought interferes a little with other activities, or wastes a little of my time.
3. *Interferes moderately.* This thought interferes with other activities, or wastes some of my time.
4. *Interferes a great deal.* This thought stops me from doing a lot of things, and wastes a lot of time everyday.

	Check here if your answer is yes	A· If yes, rate from 1 to 5	B Rate from 1 to 4
Do you worry about being on time?	_____	_____	_____
Do you worry about leaving the lights or gas on, or whether the doors are locked?	_____	_____	_____
Do you worry about your personal belongings?	_____	_____	_____
Do you worry about always keeping the house clean and tidy?	_____	_____	_____
Do you worry about keeping things in their right places?	_____	_____	_____
Do you worry about your physical health?	_____	_____	_____
Do you worry about doing things in their right order?	_____	_____	_____
Do you ever have to count things several times or go through numbers in your mind?	_____	_____	_____
Are you a person who often has a guilty conscience over quite ordinary things?	_____	_____	_____
Do unpleasant or frightening thoughts or words ever keep going over and over in your mind?	_____	_____	_____
Have you ever been troubled by certain thoughts of harming yourself or others— thoughts that come and go without any particular reason?	_____	_____	_____

	Check here if your answer is yes	A If yes, rate from 1 to 5	B Rate from 1 to 4
Do you worry about household things that might chip or splinter if they were to be knocked over or broken?	_____	_____	_____
Do you ever have persistent ideas that someone you know might be having an accident or that something might have happened to him?	_____	_____	_____
Are you preoccupied with the fear of being raped or assaulted?	_____	_____	_____
Do you go back and think about a task you have already completed, wondering how you could have done it better?	_____	_____	_____
Do you find yourself concerned with germs? ...	_____	_____	_____
Do you have to turn things over and over in your mind before being able to decide what to do?	_____	_____	_____
Do you ask yourself questions or have doubts about a lot of things that you do?	_____	_____	_____
Are there any particular things that you try to keep away from or that you avoid doing, because you know they would upset you?	_____	_____	_____

	Check here if your answer is yes	A If yes, rate from 1 to 5	B Rate from 1 to 4
Do you worry about money a lot?	_____	_____	_____
Do you frequently think that things will not get better and may, in fact, get worse?	_____	_____	_____
Do you become preoccupied with angry or irritating thoughts when people don't do things carefully or correctly?	_____	_____	_____
Do you ruminate about details?	_____	_____	_____
Do guilt-tinged memories return to you over and over?	_____	_____	_____
Do you have recurring feelings of jealousy, or fear of being abandoned?	_____	_____	_____
Do you feel nervous about heights?	_____	_____	_____
Are you at times preoccupied with the desire for things you cannot have?	_____	_____	_____
Do you worry about auto accidents?	_____	_____	_____
Do you find yourself returning to thoughts about your faults?	_____	_____	_____
Do you worry about growing old?	_____	_____	_____
Do you feel nervous when thinking about being alone?	_____	_____	_____

	Check here if your answer is yes	A If yes, rate from 1 to 5	B Rate from 1 to 4
Do you worry about dirt and/or dirty things?	_____	_____	_____
Do you tend to worry a bit about personal cleanliness or tidiness?	_____	_____	_____
Does a negative feature of your appearance or makeup preoccupy you at times?	_____	_____	_____
Do you feel that God does not accept you?	_____	_____	_____
Do you feel that you have committed the unpardonable sin?	_____	_____	_____
Do you worry about getting trapped in crowds, on bridges, in elevators? ..	_____	_____	_____
Do you think again and again about your failures?	_____	_____	_____
Sometimes do you think about your home burning?	_____	_____	_____
Do you think frequently of certain things of which you are ashamed?	_____	_____	_____
Are you preoccupied with uncomfortable thoughts about sex or sexual adequacy?	_____	_____	_____
Do you worry about God being angry at you?	_____	_____	_____

Ask these questions about each stressful thought you checked: Is the thought realistic or unrealistic? Give two examples _____

Is the thought productive or counterproductive? Give two examples _____

Is the thought neutral or self-defeating? Give two examples ____

Is the thought easy or hard to control? Give two examples ____

Ask your counselees to select a thought they feel they want to eliminate. Column A is the *discomfort rating* for each thought, while Column B is the *interference rating* for how disruptive it is to their lives. Any thought that has a discomfort rating above 3, or an interference rating above 2 may warrant thought stopping procedures.

Have them close their eyes and imagine a situation in which the stressful thought is likely to occur. Encourage your counselees to try to include normal thoughts as well as obsessive thoughts. In this way stressful thoughts can be interrupted while allowing a continuing flow of healthy thinking.

Thought Interruption

The following are suggested techniques you can use with counselees, written for them, so that you can share these things with them.

Set an egg timer or alarm for three minutes. Look away, close your eyes, and think about your stressful thought. When you hear the ring, shout, "Stop!" Do this out loud and do it twice. You may also want to raise your hand or snap your fingers or stand up. Let your mind empty of all but the neutral and nonanxious thoughts. Set a goal of about thirty seconds after the stop, during which your mind remains blank. If the upsetting thought returns during that time, shout, "Stop!" again twice.

Another approach is to write the word *stop* on a 3 × 5 card with Philippians 4:6–9.

Your next step is to take control of the thought stopping cue, but without the timer or tape recorder. While thinking about the unwanted thought, shout, "Stop!"

When you succeed in eliminating the thought on repeated attempts with the shouted command, begin countering the thought with "stop" said in a normal voice.

After you succeed in stopping the thought by using your normal speaking voice, attempt to do the same with a whisper.

When the whisper is sufficient to stop your fearful thoughts, use the command "Stop!" in your mind. Imagine shouting "Stop!" in your mind. Success at this point means that you can stop thoughts at any time and in all situations.

Thought Substitution

The last phase of thought stopping involves thought substitution. In place of the obsessive thought, make up some positive, assertive statements that are appropriate in the target situation. For example, if you are afraid of flying, you might say to yourself, "This is a fantastically beautiful view from way up here." Develop several alternative, assertive statements to say to yourself, since the same response may lose its power through repetition.

Thought Switching

When you think, imagine, daydream or fantasize, you often give yourself a set of instructions that ensures your acting in a fearful manner. These instructions soon become habits. One of the best ways to break a habit is by setting up a more powerful counterhabit. Here the counterhabit you are trying to achieve is that of teaching yourself not to be fearful. With "Thought Switching," you do not try to stop your worrisome thoughts of doom directly as you do with Thought Stoppage. Instead, you (1) select a series of counterthoughts and (2) deliberately strengthen these thoughts until they become strong enough to override or replace the anxiety thoughts. This exercise is adapted from a method devised by Dr. Lloyd Homme, a California psychologist. The purpose is to replace your fear self-instructions with positive self-instructions.

STEP ONE: The first step is to recall what you usually say prior to the fear on which you are now working. List the self-instructions you give yourself (the small, detailed ones as well as the big, overwhelming self-instructions). For example, here are the self-instructions a person who feared elevators gave himself.

1. "As I enter the building, I will start thinking about all the terrible things that can happen to me on the elevator."
2. "When I enter the building, I will strain to see if any people will be getting on the elevator with me."
3. "I will look around to make sure there is a staircase—what if I get stuck up there and I can't get back down!"
4. "I will make myself notice whether it's an express elevator or not. I will begin to wonder what if it gets stuck in the part where there are no openings."
5. "When I'm in the elevator, I will stand near the front (or the back). I will tighten my muscles and make myself think of all the bad things that might happen."
6. "I will pay attention to the slightest sound or vibration and deliberately make myself think of them as signals that things might be going wrong."

STEP TWO: For each of these self-instructions set up a list of coping self-instructions. Your aim: to set up the opposite habit of thinking so that you will be able to handle whatever happens. Here is the list that the elevator phobic worked out:

1. "As I enter the building, if I start thinking about the terrible things that might happen, I will tell myself that very little chance exists that anything bad will happen."
2. "If I find myself noticing whether people are getting on the elevator, I will tell myself that it really doesn't matter if other people are on the elevator."
3. "If I find myself searching for the staircase, I will tell myself that even if I'm nervous about coming down in the elevator, I will be able to cope with it."
4. "I will start thinking that there is very little chance of anything bad happening."
5. "When I'm on the elevator, I will deliberately relax my muscles and think about something pleasant."
6. "If I hear an unusual noise, I will tell myself that even if something goes wrong, at most it will be a minor inconvenience."

STEP THREE: Put each of the new self-instructions you have worked out for yourself on a separate card. The order doesn't matter. Carry the cards with you or stick them in a convenient place—in your purse, on top of the night table, by the telephone, etc.

STEP FOUR: Take a group of actions you perform fairly frequently every day: drinking coffee or soda, changing channels on the TV set, running a comb through your hair, washing your hands, making a phone call. Each time, just before you do one of these frequent acts, take your topmost card, read it carefully and say the instruction to yourself. Then take your first sip of coffee, turn the TV channel or run the comb through your hair. Alternate way: Say the new instruction before you do something that gives you pleasure, such as reading your mail, eating cake, watching a favorite TV program.

STEP FIVE: When you're in the real life situation, deliberately repeat the instructions and try to follow them. It may take several weeks, but your anticipatory thoughts should change and your anxiety decrease.

STEP SIX: After using your self-instructions for a while, you may think of better statements. Don't hesitate to switch, but don't change too often. You want to get enough practice with each new self-instruction so that it starts to take hold.

If you fail in your first attempt at stopping a thought it may mean that you have selected a thought that is very difficult to eliminate. Try selecting an unwanted thought that is less fearful than your initial choice. It is more important to become proficient at stopping any thought before working on the more fearful thoughts.

If saying "Stop" is not successful for you, or if you are in a public place where it would be embarrassing to say, "Stop!" aloud, you can substitute one of the following: Put a rubber band around your wrist, and when anxious thoughts occur, pull back and snap it. Or pinch yourself when the thoughts come.

Here is another approach to thought changing, which is quite simple.

1. Set aside twenty minutes for contemplation at the beginning and end of each day. Get yourself a small notebook specifically for this exercise, and during these periods of contemplation write down every worry, anxiety, concern, bothersome thought, event, or person that comes into your mind.

2. Review your list of bothersome ideas. Ask yourself, "Which of these can I take care of right now? Is there anything I can change?" Then take that action immediately and cross that concern off your list.

3. Take a moment to pray about the rest of your list—those concerns you cannot take care of there and then. Commit to God any concern you cannot change. Then close your notebook and go about your business, trusting that God is in control of all you cannot control.

4. If any concern continues to bother you, make a note of it once more in your notebook.

5. Writing down thoughts and ideas helps to get them out of your memory where they will otherwise be kept alive by the memory-refreshing mechanisms of your brain. Your notebook, therefore, serves as an external memory. It can be taken with you everywhere.

Another approach you can use to bring greater freedom from fear and a general sense of relaxation is the following tape exercise.[2] Have someone with a pleasant sounding voice tape this entire sequence, following the time designations. It might be beneficial for the counselee to record his or her own voice.

A Tape for Relaxation Therapy

You are about to enter upon an experience of relaxation and meditation. There are four requirements for a good experience.

1. *A quiet environment.* The best location will be a spot where you will not likely be disturbed. If you are, this need not prevent the experience, you can be sitting on a bus, or in some crowded place, but it will be much more effective if you can be in a situation where you will not be disturbed.

2. *A comfortable position.* Although you need a comfortable position you should not lie down because you will have a tendency to go to sleep. This is not your aim. Sleep is a different state from relaxation and not as desirable, so just make sure that you are in a place where you feel comfortable.

3. *An object to dwell on.* As you progress through this experience you'll be led by my voice and your attention will be taken through a series of stages. Ultimately you will be guided to focus on a statement from the Bible. Follow naturally after this leading.

4. *A passive attitude.* Although there will be a focal point for your thoughts, your mind may wander. Don't worry about this. Remain passive. Just gently turn your mind back to my voice. You do not have to worry about your wandering mind. This is a relaxation program. Nothing about it should worry you or raise your anxiety. (Twenty-second pause)

You do not need to worry about anything at this time. You are going to forget all about things that have worried you, bothered you, or upset you. (Twenty-second pause)

Let it be a quiet place, perhaps by the seashore where the waves are lazily rolling up on the sand, and the cool breeze is brushing your face, or in a mountain setting where you are looking out over a beautiful valley and everything looks calm and serene, or maybe in a grassy meadow, or even in your own backyard. (Twenty-second pause)

Now see yourself as actually being in your ideal place for relaxation. On the screen of your mind you are seeing all the colors, hearing the sounds, smelling the aromas. If it is a grassy field, you feel the lush grass beneath you, the warmth of the sun shining upon you, the smell of the new-mown hay; you hear the buzz of the bees. Overhead you see the fluffy white, cotton-candy clouds as they drift lazily across the blue sky. Just feel yourself enjoying the soothing, quiet, refreshing environment. (Twenty-second pause)

Feel the restfulness, the calmness of your wonderful situation, and let your whole body and mind be renewed and refreshed. (Twenty-second pause)

Now focus your attention upon your breath. Breathe deeply and evenly, deeply and evenly; think of nothing but your breath as it flows in and out of your body. (Twenty-second pause)

Say to yourself, *I am relaxing, breathing smoothly and rhythmically, fresh oxygen flows into my body; I feel calm, renewed, and refreshed.* (Twenty-second pause)

The Bible says, "Be still, and know that I am God" (Ps. 46:10). "Be still" literally means, "let your hands drop," "give up fighting." That is what I want you to do. Quit struggling. Leave yourself in the hands of God. You don't need to struggle. He will do it for you. From this time on we will follow a program of being still and relaxing. (Twenty-second pause)

Now direct your attention to the muscles of your feet and ankles. Imagine the muscles are becoming very loose and relaxed. You can let the tension and tightness flow out of your body. (Twenty-second pause)

Now let the attention focus on the calves of your legs. Imagine that they are becoming very deeply relaxed. (Twenty-second pause)

Address your attention now to the muscles in your thighs. Let the muscles become deeply relaxed, just let go and let the muscles of your legs become completely relaxed. (Twenty-second pause)

As your hip muscles are becoming more and more relaxed let your attention shift to the muscles in your abdomen and your lower back. Let the muscles become very relaxed, all the time breathing in peace and relaxation, and breathing out tension, tightness, and anxiety.

Let your attention move to your chest muscles and the muscles in your upper back. Once again, let those muscles become very relaxed. With each breath you are becoming very deeply relaxed. (Twenty-second pause)

Now take time to concentrate on the muscles in your arms and shoulders. Let your shoulder muscles relax, beginning with your upper arms and descending down through each finger in your hands. You are becoming very relaxed. (Twenty-second pause)

Think of your muscles as being bound with a tourniquet. The tourniquet is holding your muscles tight. Release it. Feel all your muscles go loose. (Twenty-second pause)

You are now deeply relaxed—more deeply relaxed than you have been any time today. (Twenty-second pause)

Take just a moment to survey the muscles of your body. If you note any place where there is tightness, let the tightness flow out of your body with your next breath. (Twenty-second pause)

Concentrate upon the circulatory system of your body. See it as a pipeline carrying the life-giving blood to all the vital parts of your body. Envisage the Alaska pipeline as it comes across the snowy wastes, carrying oil to the energy-thirsty forty-eight states. See the maintenance men guarding those pipes and their precious contents. Notice the way they work to make sure that the oil continues to flow on its way to the places where it is badly needed. Sense your blood moving through your circulatory system to every part of your body, bringing life-giving oxygen and energy. (Twenty-second pause)

Continue to focus on your breath as it flows in and out. Remember that oxygen is bringing life to your bloodstream and your heart. The Bible refers to God's Spirit as the breath of God. Feel the breath of God's Spirit entering your body. (Twenty-second pause)

We are now embarking on a program of Christian meditation. Our theme is taken from the prophecy of Isaiah. "They who wait for the Lord shall renew their strength, they shall mount up with wings like eagles, they shall run and not be weary, they shall walk and not faint" (Isa. 40:31). (Twenty-second pause)

We are now turning to a statement from the New Testament: "I can do all things through Christ which strengtheneth me" (Phil. 4:13 KJV). (Twenty-second pause)

Continue to breathe deeply and evenly. As you breathe in, say within yourself, "I can do all things."

As you breathe out repeat, "through Christ which strengtheneth me." (Twenty-second pause)

Be calm, be patient, put all your thoughts aside and concentrate on: "I can do all things through Christ which strengtheneth me." (Twenty-second pause)

Don't let anything in your mind interrupt your focus on this statement: "I can do all things through Christ which strengtheneth me." (Twenty-second pause)

Think again of your circulatory system. See your arteries and your veins as tubes carrying your blood to all parts of your body. See these tubes with clamps on them. The clamps are restricting the flow of the life-giving blood. Now visualize the clamps being released. Let them go—release them so your blood can flow without any restriction. The life-giving blood is flowing through your body. (Twenty-second pause)

Be aware of what you are thinking, all the time conscious of accessions of strength. "I can do all things through Christ which strentheneth me." (Twenty-second pause)

Forget all the distractions that would turn your mind aside and repeat, "I can do all things through Christ which strengtheneth me."

If you feel you are becoming drowsy or your mind is racing, turn it back and repeat, "I can do all things through Christ which strengtheneth me." (Twenty-second pause)

Envisage your circulatory system again. See it now like irrigation channels leading all over your body. As the life-giving liquid flows across the desert, see your blood flowing into every part of your body. (Twenty-second pause)

Let all your cares drop from you like some clothing you removed and dropped to the floor, and recall, "I can do all things through Christ which strengtheneth me." (Twenty-second pause)

Continue to breathe deeply and evenly, deeply and evenly, and repeat, "I can do all things through Christ which strengtheneth me." (Twenty-second pause)

Continue to see the blood flowing freely through your body without any restriction upon it as you grow more and more relaxed. Your blood is flowing through your circulatory system. (Twenty-second pause)

Now open your eyes. Rest quietly for a moment and then move into the joy of what awaits you in God's wonderful day.

APPENDIX 2

BIBLIOGRAPHY

Beck, A. T. *Cognitive Therapy and the Emotional Disorders.* New York: International Universities Press, 1976. Paperbound edition published by New American Library, New York, 1979.

_____. *Depression: Clinical, Experimental and Theoretical Aspects.* New York: Harper and Row, 1967. Republished as *Depression: Causes and Treatment.* Philadelphia: University of Pennsylvania Press, 1972.

Beck, A. T. and Emery, Gary. *Anxiety Disorders and Phobias.* New York: Basic Books, 1985.

_____. "Cognitive Therapy of Anxiety and Phobic Disorders. Unpublished manuscript, 1979.

Beck, A. T., Rush, A. J., Shaw, B. F., and Emery G. *Cognitive Therapy of Depression.* New York: Guilford Press, 1979.

Burns, D. *Feeling Good: The New Mood Therapy.* New York: William Morrow and Company, 1980.

Crabb, Lawrence J., Jr. *Effective Biblical Counseling.* Grand Rapids: Zondervan, 1977.

Emery, Gary, Hollon, Steven D. and Bedrosian, Richard C. eds. *New Directions in Cognitive Therapy.* New York: Guilford Press, 1981.

Gauthier, J. and Marshall, W. L. "Grief: A Cognitive Behavioral Analysis," *Cognitive Therapy and Research* (1977):39–44.

Goldstein, A. P., Heller, E. and Sechrest, L. B. *Psychotherapy and the Psychology of Behavior Change.* New York: Wiley, 1966.

Kendall, P. "On the Efficacious Use of Verbal-Instructional Procedures with Children," *Cognitive Therapy and Research* (1977):331–341.

Klerman, G.L., Rounsaville, B., Chevron, E., Nev, C., and Weissman, M. "Manual for Short-term Interpersonal Psychotherapy of Depression." Unpublished Manuscript, 1979.

Meichenbaum, D. *Cognitive-Behavior Modification.* New York: Plenum Press, 1977.

Schmidt, Jerry A. *Do You Hear What You're Thinking?* Wheaton, Ill.: Victor Books, 1983.

Spivack, G., Platt, S., and Shute, M. *The Problem-Solving Approach to Adjustment.* San Francisco: Jossey-Bass, 1976.

Stoop, David. *Self-Talk: Key to Personal Growth.* Old Tappan, N.J.: Fleming H. Revell, 1982.

Wright, H. Norman. *Crisis Counseling.* San Bernardino, Calif.: Here's Life Publishers, 1985.

Books on Neuro-linguistic Programming:

Practical Magic: A Translation of Basic Neuro-linguistic Programming into Clinical Psychotherapy. Stephen R. Lankton (Meta Publications, 1980, P.O. Box 565, Cupertino, CA 95015.

The original books on this subject are *The Structure of Magic, Volumes I* and *II* (1975). Richard Bandler and John Grinder, Science and Behavior Books, Palo Alto, Calif.

The most practical resource has been *The Magic of Rapport* by Jerry Richardson and Joel Margolis, Harbor Publishers, San Francisco. This book has been out of print for some time, but may be available in used bookstores or libraries. It is worth discovering.

Books to use to help men with their emotions:

Why Am I Afraid To Tell You Who I Am? (1969) and *Why Am I Afraid to Love?* (1972) by John Powell (Argus Publications).

The Secrets Men Keep. Dr. Ken Druck with James C. Simmons (Garden City: Doubleday & Company, 1985).

NOTES

Chapter 1. The Most Important Element in Counseling

1. D. Corydon Hammond, Dean H. Hepworth, and Veon G. Smith, *Improving Therapeutic Communication* (San Francisco: Jossey-Bass, 1977), 114, 115.

2. Robert Dilts, *Applications of Neuro-Linguistic Programming*, (Cupertino, Calif.: Meta Publications, 1983), 5 adapted.

3. Ibid., 9 adapted.

Chapter 2. Hazards in Counseling

1. Adapted from Gerald Corey and Marianne Schneider Corey, *Issues and Ethics in the Helping Professions* (Monterey, Calif.: Brooks Cole Publishing Co., 1984), 111.

2. Adapted from Corey and Corey, 33, 34.

Chapter 3. Thought Life—The Foundation for Counseling

1. Maurice Wagner, *The Sensation of Being Somebody* (Grand Rapids: Zondervan, 1975), 164.

2. Lloyd Ahlem, *Do I Have To Be Me?* (Ventura, Calif.: Regal Books, 1973), 71.

3. J. I. Packer, *Knowing God* (Downers Grove, Ill.: InterVarsity Press, 1973), 37.

4. Some material adapted from "Cognitive Theory/Therapy and Sanctification: A Study in Integration," by David Pecheur, *Journal of Psychology and Theology*, Fall 1978, 6(4), 239–253; and "Effective Counseling and Psychotherapy: An Integrative Review of Research" by Keith J. Edwards, *Journal of Psychology and Theology*, 94, 107.

5. Charles Swindoll, *Come Before Winter* (Portland, Ore.: Multnomah Press, 1985), 239.

Chapter 4. The Inner Conversation Approach to Counseling

1. Concepts in this section are adapted from three sources. Matthew McKay, Martha Davis, and Patrick Fanning, *Thoughts and Feelings* (Richmond, Calif.: New Harbinger Publications, 1981), 19–27; Aaron T. Beck, *Cognitive Therapy and the Emotional Disorders* (New York: International Universities Press, 1976); David D. Burns, *Feeling Good* (New York: William Morrow and Company, 1980).

2. John Lembo, *The Counseling Process* (Roslyn Heights, N.Y.: Libra, 1976), 20, 21 adapted.

3. See *Crisis Counseling* by the author, published by Here's Life Publishers, San Bernardino, Calif.

4. Aaron T. Beck and Gary Emery, *Anxiety Disorders and Phobias* (New York: Basic Books, 1985), 171, 172 adapted.

5. Ibid., 177.

6. Ibid., 183.

Chapter 5. Helping People Change Their Thought Lives

1. *Making Peace With Your Past,* by the author, is published by Fleming H. Revell (1984).

2. This chart is given in *Crisis Counseling* by the author, published by Here's Life Publishers (1985).

3. Gary Emery, *A New Beginning:* How You Can Change Your Thoughts Through Cognitive Therapy (New York: Simon and Schuster, 1981), 61.

4. Ibid., adapted.

5. John Lembo, D. W. Johnson, and R. P. Matross, "Attitude Modification Methods" in *Helping People Change: A Textbook of Methods,* eds. F. H. Kanfer and A. P. Goldstein (Elsford, N.Y.: Pergamon Press, 1975), 65 adapted.

6. Lembo, 107 adapted.

Chapter 6. The Use of Imagery in Counseling

1. Vincent Collins, *Me, Myself and You* (St. Meinard, Ind.: Abbey Press, 1974), 30.

2. Alexander Whyte: as quoted by Hannah Hurnard, *Winger Life.* Used by permission from Artype Services, Portland, Oregon.

3. Alan Richardson, *Mental Imagery* (New York: Springer Pub., 1969), 56 adapted.

4. G. Leonard, *The Ultimate Athlete* (New York: Avon Books, 1977), 115, 116 adapted.

5. C. A. Garfield, "How to Achieve Peak Performance," paper presented at a workshop. San Francisco, May 1981, and T. Gallway and B. Kriegel, *Inner Skiing* (New York: Random House, 1977), 119 adapted.

6. Adapted from H. Norman Wright, *Making Peace With Your Past,* 54.

7. See Errol R. Korn and Karen Johnson Dow, *Visualization— The Uses of Imagery in the Health Professions* (Homewood, Ill.: Jones-Irwin, 1983).

8. John Lembo, 66 adapted.

9. Richard M. Suinn, *Fundamentals of Behavior Pathology* (New York: Wiley, 1970), 308–310 adapted.

10. David Seamands, *The Healing of Memories* (Wheaton, Ill.: Victor Books, 1985), 67, 68.

11. Aaron T. Beck and Gary Emery, 213.

12. Suinn.

Chapter 7. The Untapped Resource of Counseling—Prayer

1. John Baillie, *A Diary of Private Prayer* (London: Oxford University Press, 1936), 73.

2. Ibid., 11.

3. J. I. Packer, *Knowing God* (Downer's Grove, Ill.: InterVarsity Press, 1973).

4. J. B. Phillips, *Your God Is Too Small* (New York: Macmillan, 1962).

5. Lloyd John Ogilvie, *Praying with Power* (Ventura, Calif.: Regal Books, 1983), 56, 57.

6. Lewis B. Smedes, *How Can It Be All Right When Everything Is All Wrong?* (New York: Harper and Row, 1983), 3.

7. Don Baker, *Pain's Hidden Purpose* (Portland, Ore.: Multnomah Press, 1984), 72.

8. Lloyd John Ogilvie, *Why Not? Accept Christ's Healing and Wholeness* (Old Tappan, N.J.: Fleming H. Revell, 1985), 162.

9. Larry Richards, *When It Hurts Too Much To Wait* (Waco, Tex.: Word, 1985), 67, 68.

10. Lloyd John Ogilvie, *God's Will in Your Life* (Eugene, Ore.: Harvest House, 1982), 144, 145.

Chapter 8. Practical Applications

1. Suggested reading on the subject of depression includes *Depression, Coping and Caring,* by Archibald Hart (Cope Publications), *Counseling the Depressed,* by Hart (to be published by Word Books in 1987 as a part of the Resources for Christian Counseling series), and *Now I Know Why I'm Depressed,* by the author (Harvest House).

2. Aaron T. Beck, *Depression: Causes and Treatment* (Philadelphia: University of Pennsylvania Press, 1972).

3. Aaron T. Beck, *Cognitive Therapy,* 271–273.

4. Ibid., 283, 4, adapted.

5. Richard F. Berg and Christine McCartney, *Depression and the Integrated Life* (New York: Alba House, 1981), 141.

6. David Burns, *Feeling Good: The New Mood Therapy* (New York: William Morrow and Company, 1980), 319, 20.

7. Les Carter, *The Push-Pull Marriage* (Grand Rapids: Baker Book House, 1983), 63, adapted.

8. Burns, 141–147 adapted.

9. Ibid., 135–177.

10. Ibid., 150.

11. H. Norman Wright, *The Rights and Wrongs of Anger* (Eugene, Ore.: Harvest House, 1985), 92–108, adapted.

Appendix 1. Suggested Methods for Controlling Thoughts

1. Martha Davis, et al., *The Relaxation and Stress Reduction Workbook* (Richmond, Calif.: New Harbinger Publications, 1980), 93–95, adapted from the Leyton Scale.

2. John Drakeford, *The Awesome Power of the Healing Thought* (Nashville: Broadman, 1981).

INDEX

H. Norman Wright

H. Norman Wright is a licensed Marriage, Family, and Child Therapist. He holds an M.R.E. from Fuller Theological Seminary, an M.A. in Clinical Psychology from Pepperdine University and an honorary doctorate from Western Conservative Baptist Seminary. For seven years, he served as a minister of education and youth in a local church and for over twenty years has taught at the Talbot Graduate School of Theology. For several of these years, he taught and directed the Graduate Department of Marriage, Family, and Child Therapy at Biola University. Presently, he maintains a private practice and conducts training seminars for ministers throughout the U.S.A. He is the author of over forty-five books and is the founder and director of Christian Marriage Enrichment and Family Counseling and Enrichment in Santa Ana, California. He lives in Long Beach with his wife Joycelin and is the father of a daughter Sheryl and a son Matthew.